COACH YOURSELF TO WIN

COACH YOURSELF TO WIN

Seven Steps to Breakthrough Performance on the Job and in Your Life

HOWARD M. GUTTMAN

McGraw Hill

New York Chicago San Francisco Lisbon
London Madrid Mexico City Milan New Delhi
San Juan Seoul Singapore Sydney Toronto

The McGraw-Hill Companies

1 2 3 4 5 6 7 8 9 0 WFR/WFR 1 5 4 3 2 1 0

ISBN 978-0-07-164034-3
MHID 0-07-164034-7

Library of Congress Cataloging-in-Publication Data
Guttman, Howard M.
Coach yourself to win : seven steps to breakthrough performance on the job and in your life / by Howard M. Guttman.
p. cm.
Includes bibliographical references and index.
ISBN 978-0-07-164034-3 (alk. paper)
1. Success in business. 2. Change (Psychology) 3. Self-actualization (Psychology) 4. Personal coaching I. Title.
HF5386.G88 2011
650.1--dc22

2010026259

CONTENTS

Preface vii

Acknowledgments xi

Before We Begin xiii

Introduction Ready, Set—Now Coach Yourself to Win. . . . 1

Chapter 1 Can You Coach Yourself to Win? 17

Action Steps:
1.1 Are You in It for the Long Haul? 36
1.2 Are You Able to Change Your Behavior? 38
1.3 Are You Ready to Change Your Behavior? 38
1.4 Are You Self-Coachable 39

Chapter 2 Setting Your Intention 43

Action Steps:
2.1 What Is Your Intention? 74
2.2 To Whom Will You Declare Your Intention? 74
2.3 What Are Your Stories and Where Do They Come From? 75
2.4 Evaluate Your Stories. .75
2.5 Write Up Your Stories' "P&L Statements" 76
2.6 Write Your "New You" Stories 76
2.7 What's Your First Step? 76

Chapter 3 Choosing Your Traveling Companions 77

Action Steps:
3.1 Who Will Be Your Guide? 109
3.2 Discussing Your Intention with Your Guide . . .109
3.3 Who Will Be in Your Circle of Support? 109

Chapter 4 What's the Message? 111

Action Steps:

4.1 Questions for Your Guide and Circle of Support 127

4.2 Briefing Packet for Your Guide and Circle of Support 127

Chapter 5 How Should You Respond? 137

Action Step:

5.1 Creating Your Discussion Plan 153

Chapter 6 Mapping Your Route 155

Action Steps:

6.1 Stories about Planning. 181

6.2 Writing SMART Objectives 181

6.3 Creating Your Personal Development Plan (PDP) 182

6.4 Communicating Your Plan to Your Circle of Support 183

Chapter 7 Getting and Staying There 187

Notes 213

Additional Resources for Self-Coachees 219

Index 249

PREFACE

"A lawyer who represents himself has a fool for a client." It's a time-tested truism in the legal profession. Could the same be true for self-coaching? Would someone who is adventurous enough to try to coach him- or herself be equally foolish? Should coaching, whether in the business world or in everyday life, be left in the hands of professionals, those whose names are followed by imposing initials that signify that they've passed some litmus test of professional respectability?

As someone who has spent more than 20 years leading an organization that coaches hundreds of executives each year, I can hardly be accused of undervaluing the art and discipline of coaching. Coaching is a profession that takes skill, experience, and insight into human behavior. Whether it is designed to deal with problematic individuals or (as I've seen with increasing frequency in recent years) to help executives improve their game, coaching requires a deep understanding of how to bring about lasting behavioral modification.

But it is also true that there are millions of people "out there," both in the business world and in everyday life, who for one reason or another cannot or choose not to avail themselves of the services of a professional coach. A first-line supervisor, buried deep within the organization, may want to improve his game but, alas, management provides coaches only for those who are farther up the ladder. A longtime stay-at-home parent may want to reenter the workforce but can't afford the services of a career counselor. An overweight individual may be too uncomfortable to wage a public battle of the bulge.

Coach Yourself to Win is written for the vast number of people who want to create a new future for themselves, either by modifying or changing behavior that is hindering them or by adopting new, more productive habits to improve their performance on the job or in their life. One key premise of the book is that the first place to turn to achieve your Intention—your commitment to achieve an end result—is not to some outside agency or program, but inward, to *yourself*. Change is, first and foremost, an *interior* game; you are the star player. Self-coaching is a way for you to undertake the process of self-discovery and self-mastery, enabling you to achieve, as suggested by the subtitle of this book, breakthrough performance on the job and in your life.

A second premise relates to change and choice. Personal change is something that occurs in one of two basic ways: it happens either by chance or by choice. I grew up in Newark, New Jersey, in the 1960s. I had friends who grew up in the inner city, which had some very tough areas. There was a sense among many who lived there that they were at the mercy of larger forces, over which they exercised little or no control. In their mind, personal change was not a matter of choice; it was completely outside their control. Not surprisingly, some of these people never escaped the confines of inner-city Newark.

I certainly do not subscribe to this way of thinking. I believe that, short of deep-seated psychological or emotional impediments to self-improvement (which require the intervention of a psychologist or psychiatrist), most of us are capable of moving from where we are now to a brighter future. We *can* achieve our Intention—the "happy ending" that we desire. But being capable is one thing; having the will is another. In Chapter 2, I point to Intention as the driving force for personal change and the pivot point for the self-coaching process. Without a deeply felt Intention, it's unlikely that you will be able to break away from your past, no matter how desperately you want to leave it behind.

The third premise of the book sets it apart from most of the "self-help" volumes that you are likely to encounter: *self-coaching is not something that you do by yourself.* While you are the captain of your future, the journey to a New You requires you to take along some traveling companions. One of the seven steps in this self-coaching process is the enrollment of a team of people—a Guide and a Circle of Support—who know you well, care about your well-being, and are committed to helping you realize your Intention. Their participation will make your journey less of a high-wire act and more of a collaborative undertaking. Think of them as the safety net that will support you as you strive for your Intention.

This book represents a unique undertaking. While many self-help books offer advice on how to improve either your career or your personal life, we bridge the two worlds in order to help our readers improve their performance, whether they are earning their living or living their life. In thinking about adapting the executive-coaching process to your use on and off your job, I asked two questions: "What are the best practices in coaching?" and "How can these be put into the hands of a broad number of people so that they can effectively apply them to a wide variety of concerns, whether these involve careers and professional success or personal well-being and home life?"

The seven-step self-coaching process that you will be exposed to in *Coach Yourself to Win* is an adaptation of the best practices that my colleagues and I have used in executive coaching for more than 20 years. It has been proven to work with one of the most challenging groups of people: high-powered, strong-willed businesspeople whose careers and whose financial and professional success hinge on their ability to change. Their success is proof of the soundness of the process—a process that can significantly increase your chances of fulfilling your Intention.

But self-coaching is more than mastering mechanics. Not everyone is suited to self-coaching, which is why, in Chapter 1, we ask you to evaluate whether or not you are *able, ready, and willing to permanently change your behavior*. Nor can everyone be authentically committed to actualizing her Intention, regardless of the benefits, or to reaching out to acquaintances for feedback and support. But for those who can, the rewards are many and often life-changing. So, why not turn the page and begin taking seven steps that will enable you to *Coach Yourself to Win*?

ACKNOWLEDGMENTS

My heartfelt thanks to Jackie Guttman, my business partner and partner in life, for the invaluable insights, critique, and support that she provided me during the writing of this book.

I'm indebted to Dale Corey and Peter M. Tobia for their competent and caring editorial support.

To Barbara Becker, Marty Becker, Monica Sobon, Dr. Alan Stavitsky, and Dr. Annette Tobia, many thanks for your thorough and honest feedback.

Finally, I owe great thanks to all my colleagues at Guttman Development Strategies who for over 20 years have applied our coaching process to elevate the performance, effectiveness, and sense of well-being of thousands of executives around the world.

BEFORE WE BEGIN . . .

A unique aspect of *Coach Yourself to Win* is its interactive nature. After each step in the self-coaching process has been explained and illustrated with real-life examples, you will be asked to think about how that step relates to you and your Intention.

Action Steps—the kind of thinking that you need to do and the questions that you need to answer—appear at the end of each chapter, and the point at which each step should be completed is indicated in the chapter.

We have created a special Web site for you: www.coachyourselftowin.com. There you will find a number of forms and questionnaires related to each Action Step, which you can download and save on your computer. As you take each step, you can complete the saved form, drafting your response on paper first or typing it directly into the form.

Ways in which your Guide and your Circle of Support can utilize the Web site throughout the process are explained in Chapter 4.

Share this book with the person whom you choose to be your Guide. It will deepen his or her understanding of the rationale behind each step and will enable the two of you to work in close collaboration and partnership. It would be helpful for the members of your Circle of Support to read the book as well. In "Additional Resources for Self-Coachees," which are included in the book and on the Web site, we have gathered information on organizations, other Web sites, and publications related to specific goals: overcoming addictions, dealing with health problems, changing careers, improving your on-the-job performance, and so on. Depending on the results you are seeking from your self-coaching experience, you may find additional support from one or more of these resources.

Now, let's begin our journey.

READY, SET—NOW COACH YOURSELF TO WIN

The Self-Coaching Process
1 Determine Your Self-Coachability
2 Select and Commit to an Intention
3 Identify Your Guide and Circle of Support
4 Solicit Feedback
5 Analyze and Respond to Feedback
6 Develop and Act on a Game Plan
7 Track Your Success and Recalibrate

Oprah Winfrey is probably the best-known dieter in the world. For more than 20 years, viewers and the tabloid press all over the world have watched her weight yo-yo up and down. Back in 1988, they applauded her success when she lost 67 pounds on a liquid-protein diet. Two years later, they commiserated when she announced that she'd gained back all the weight and "would never diet again."

By 1992, Oprah's weight had gone up to 237 pounds, and she went on another diet. This time she did it more sensibly, combining low-calorie meals with lots of exercise, particularly running. By 1994, she had dropped the weight and had run a marathon. It looked as though she had won the battle until a year later, when the weight started inching back. In 1996, she hired personal trainer Bob Greene, saying that at last her "roller-coaster weight saga" was over. She remained active and fit for a number of years, but she eventually began regaining weight, and by 2004 she was back up to 240 pounds.

She once again made weight loss a public goal, dropping 80 pounds and appearing on the January 2005 cover of *O* magazine at a toned 160 pounds. "I thought I was finished with the weight battle," she wrote earlier this year. "I was done. I'd conquered it. I was so sure . . ."[1]

In the January 2009 issue of *O*, Oprah confessed that she had reached the 200-pound mark again. "I'm mad at myself," she wrote. "I'm embarrassed. . . . I can't believe that after all these years, all the things I know how to do, I'm still talking about my weight."[2]

Moving from talk to setting an Intention—*and staying in that Intention*—is no easy task, as Oprah has discovered. Oprah, of course, is an experienced dieter. She probably qualifies for a Ph.D. in the subject. But despite a support group that numbers in the millions, the best coaches that money can buy, and a spotlight fixed glaringly on her every pound, she has not yet mastered the ability to lose weight permanently.

Oprah is no different from many of us. We set goals, we reach, we grasp—and then we fall back on old habits. We remain down on ourselves for a while, until we muster up the courage to begin anew, only to have the cycle repeat itself.

It's not initiating change that is so challenging, though Lord knows it is tough enough to do so. Rather, *it is proceeding from Intention to sustained behavior change.* I know, from both personal and professional experience, that *permanently replacing deeply ingrained behaviors with new ones* is one of the hardest challenges to overcome.

Look at a few statistics. An estimated 438,000 Americans die each year from diseases caused by smoking. Smoking is actually responsible for an estimated one in five U.S. deaths.[3] Addiction to food is another major killer: obesity is closely linked with heart disease, stroke, diabetes, and certain cancers. Yet, in America over the last two decades, adult obesity rates doubled, from 15 to 30 percent, and only 31 percent of American adults report engaging in regular leisure-time physical activity.[4] This despite considerable research that links lack of exercise to impaired cognitive, psychological, and physical function. Concludes Dr. Jennifer B. McClure, "Nearly half of the leading causes of death in our society are attributable to modifiable behaviors such as unhealthy diet; sedentary lifestyle; using tobacco, drugs, or alcohol; and failure to get screened for cancer."[5]

The huge number of people who ignore the statistics and continue to smoke, overeat, spend their free time in front of the TV, and engage in countless other unhealthy lifestyles is a telltale indicator that old habits die hard—and that we will continue to die fast. The "forever" makeover is indeed the Mt. Everest of personal challenges.

But it can be done. People do succeed in changing their own behavior, not just temporarily, but for the rest of their lives. Many people with serious weight problems—think Richard "Sweatin' to the Oldies" Simmons and Weight Watchers' founder Jean Nidetch—have succeeded where Oprah has failed. Shrinking violets become toastmasters; stock boys become CEOs; stringers become star athletes; abusive spouses become supportive partners; entrepreneurs create empires. Every day, people who once saw themselves as losers become winners. They go from being mad at themselves and embarrassed by their failures to possessing a new sense of self-esteem and real pride in their accomplishments.

If unlimited resources are not the answer, nor is access to celebrity coaches and trainers or a cheering section that numbers in the millions, what is the secret to permanent behavior change? What separates those who make it to the top of the mountain from those who get stuck on the uphill climb and those who, like Oprah, no sooner reach the pinnacle than they backslide?

Now let's move from Oprah and everyone else to *you*: What keeps *you* from reaching *your* personal and professional goals? What "new you" do you want to become? And how can you take control of your behavior and command your future by relying on your own internal resources and a small team of supporters?

These are the questions that we will answer in the pages that follow. After more than 20 years of personally coaching some of the toughest cases—executives with big jobs and even bigger challenges, whose workplace behavior ranged from passive to aggressive and everything in between—I have concluded that there is a pathway that is sure to lead to *lasting behavior change*, whether the change you seek is in the workplace or in your life space. This book describes that pathway and provides the guidance that you will need if you are to coach yourself to win.

Every author has a bias. Let me share mine before we walk together along the pathway to sustained behavior change. I believe that:

- **People can and do make—and remake—themselves**. As tough as it is to change for good, it can be done. History offers countless examples of individuals and even societies that have undergone sweeping, revolutionary change. But there's no need to look back to St. Augustine or Mahatma Gandhi to prove the point. Just walk over to the nearest AA meeting to discover ordinary people who have chosen to change their lives forever by overcoming serious addiction.

- **Change begins with making choices.** There are many theories that attempt to explain human behavior and change. Original sin; the Freudian triangulation of id, ego, and superego; and the social or economic determinism posited by Marx and others quickly come to mind. However valid these theories may be, I believe that, ultimately, change at a personal level involves a fundamental choice. *You can choose how you behave.* By setting your Intention, as we will see in Chapter 2, you can trigger a process of reflecting, imagining, willing and, ultimately, acting.
- **Behavior is what counts.** As an executive coach, I help people reach their goals by helping them change their behavior. This differs from psychology and psychiatry, which attempt to change the "inner self." These disciplines deal with emotions and deep-seated feelings, and, after you read Chapter 1, you may want to put down this book and consult a psychiatrist or psychologist before you travel along our pathway to personal change. *Our focus is on how you behave, not why you do so*; on how you "show up" to those around you, not the complex of feelings and emotions that are embedded within you.
- **Self-coaching can help you achieve lasting behavior change**. This book is designed to help you attain the goals that are important to you. Your goal may be to improve your performance—on the job, in a sport, or at a hobby. It may be to improve the way you relate to the significant others in your life. Or it may be to improve yourself—to get healthier, shed bad habits, or become a "new you," however you choose to define this. No matter what your Intention, we have found that the same process we use to transform executive performance can be applied to help you perform better in all aspects of your life. Self-coaching is an especially exciting and effective

pathway to personal change because *you* ultimately become accountable for your success. There is nowhere to hide, no finger-pointing.

Don't be intimidated. In a sense, the self-reliance feature of self-coaching is also present when you engage a third-party therapist or coach. As Dr. Albert Ellis once observed, "Indeed, you really require self-analysis for *any* basic personality change. For even if you receive competent therapeutic help, unless you add your *own* persistent and forceful self-analysis, you will tend to superficially and unlastingly improve."[6]

- **Self-coaching begins with the thought: yes, I can**. Let's assume, before you are put to the test in the next chapter, that you have made a leap of faith and believe that, "Yes, you can." Your next step is to set the stage for success. Pretend that you are an actor or actress in a new movie, with you in the starring role. You want to be sure that all the elements are in place for you to become a star performer. Since this movie involves coaching yourself to win, there are three "must" preconditions that you will want to be sure are in place. If they are not, there's no point in rolling the film. If they are in place, then you can move on to take the *seven steps to breakthrough performance*. And, if you follow these steps in good faith, it's highly likely that you will be successful in reaching your goals and will win at achieving sustained behavior change.

THE THREE PRECONDITIONS

Let's take a look at each of the three preconditions, or "must" factors, that you need in order to successfully coach yourself to win.

1. Accurate data—so that you understand the current "actual" and what winning looks like

In our business coaching, we are often called in to help an executive who is doing quite well but would like to take his performance to a higher level. At other times, we are called in after a person's boss, peers, or subordinates have identified behaviors that are interfering with his ability to accomplish his business goals. In either case, the person's manager or a human resources professional briefs us on the situation and provides us with initial data.

In subsequent interviews with the person (the potential *coachee*), if we determine that he is coachable, we use a number of qualitative and quantitative tools, which will be discussed in detail in Chapter 4, to gather more detailed information on the situation.

A similar approach works well for those who want to raise their performance rating, even without a mandate from above. The businessperson who is committed to self-coaching can easily solicit feedback from colleagues. Some of the tools that we just mentioned can be adapted by self-coachees who want help identifying behaviors that they can modify or eliminate in order to become better at their job: Do they need to speak up more at meetings? Lead by influencing rather than commanding? Become more politically savvy? Deliver on promises? Learn to be less sensitive to feedback? If you assure your coworkers that their candid feedback will not be resented, but will be valued and acted on, chances are that you'll get an unvarnished and very useful picture of the level on which you need to change.

It's not nearly so easy when a person decides to be her own *life* coach. Unless and until a person knows and is able to validate what she chooses to accomplish—what Intention she should really be striving for—the effort is bound to be misdirected and ultimately fail.

The self-coachee may be willing to admit to himself that there's a problem, but what is the extent of that problem? A person who drinks three martinis every night may agree that that's two too many. He may resolve to cut back to one before dinner, but isn't he just fooling himself? Won't that one soon become two, and the two become three, and soon he'll be right back where he started? Unless he admits, from the beginning, that once he starts drinking he can't stop, and therefore he shouldn't have even one drink, his attempt to change his behavior will fail.

When you sign on for self-coaching, you need the equivalent of the boss, peers, and subordinates. You need other people to give you an objective picture of your actual behavior and how it is interfering with your ability to meet your goals. So, if you are the three-martini guy and you tell your friends about your plans to cut back to one drink a night, you will no doubt get a large dose of reality. They will probably point out that one drink has never been enough for you in the past, so why do you think it will be this time? The data will come in pretty directly: you need to stop drinking altogether. From an *objective* point of view, that's what success would look like for you.

Or perhaps you are a recently divorced individual who is preoccupied with finding another mate. Maybe your efforts are concentrated on improving your appearance and traveling in circles where you would be likely to meet an eligible prospect. It's not an off-the-wall strategy, but have you stopped to think about why your previous relationship deteriorated? If you had, you just might have realized that at least part of the problem could lie with your being wrapped up only in yourself and your interests. Working on your outer self isn't going to improve your behavior or get you another mate. If you were serious about changing your life for the better, you would do some soul-searching and solicit feedback from friends. While there are some things that even your best friend won't tell you, there are others that only she can.

2. A "Guide" in the loop: someone who is in a position to observe your progress and help you stay on track

Here again, executives who are encouraged by management to attend coaching sessions have an advantage over those who are seeking coaching on their own. As I have explained, our initial information about a potential coachee usually comes from a third party: the boss or a member of the HR function. In effect, this person is the mentor, or Guide: the point person throughout the coaching, who receives updates from the coach and coachee and helps them over rough spots in the road.

If you are a businessperson who is embarking on a self-coaching program, we recommend that you ask a trusted colleague to play this role, as it is a critically important one. Without a Guide, especially when you are your own coach, it's easy to derail and not know how to get back on track. As an observer who is on the scene yet remains objective, your Guide can spot trouble in its earliest stages and recommend adjustments to your plan.

A Guide is equally important when you are coaching yourself toward a personal goal. There are some people who try to reach their goal without this support. You have no doubt seen commercials featuring Jared, "the Subway Guy," who devised his own daily diet of two Subway sandwiches, baked potato chips, and diet soda when he weighed 425 pounds. He didn't tell anyone what he was doing until his best friend noticed that he had lost weight. By the time it became apparent to his family, and he weighed himself for the first time, he had dropped 94 pounds. From then on, his friend and family became staunch supporters and did everything they could to help him reach his ultimate goal of 180 pounds. Jared says that he didn't tell anyone about his diet until he had gotten significant results because when he had failed in the past he had disappointed others and felt terrible about it.[7]

Postscript: Jared kept the weight off for 10 years, but recent reports are that he has started to put it back on. To regain control, we suggest that this time around he start by selecting a Guide to help him get back—and stay—on track.

For most people who do not tell anyone about their commitment to a self-improvement program, "going it alone" just makes it easier to give up. There's no one to disappoint but yourself, so when the going gets tough you've got an easy out.

While I don't endorse shouting from the rooftops that you are going to lose 100 pounds or run a marathon or get a job that pays $30,000 more than your current one, I do believe that you need to make your Intention at least semipublic. Traveling solo along the pathway to self-change can be a lonely trip. It's better to open the dialogue between self and soul to others whom you trust.

Ask someone to witness your commitment to a goal and help you achieve it. Whomever you choose as your Guide—whether it's a coworker, relative, friend, or spouse—the selection criteria are the same as those used by management when assigning a mentor to an employee who is going through professional coaching. You need to identify someone who is in a position to assess your progress on a regular basis as you try to move your game ahead with new, positive actions. And that person needs to be completely honest, willing to hold up the mirror so that you can view yourself, warts and all, as you set your Intention to change.

Your Guide also needs to be able to view the situation as objectively as possible, so, in selecting the person, beware of possible conflicts of interest. If you've got your sights set on the sales manager position, don't ask another salesperson, who may have a vested interest in the outcome, to guide you. If you are trying to resolve your differences with your brother, don't ask your mother to be your Guide.

As an executive coach, I think of my relationship to the executive I'm coaching as that of navigator to driver. When all is said and done, it's the coachee's journey. He is in the driver's seat; I'm there to suggest the best route, point out roadblocks and hazards along the way, and keep him from going off the road. Your Guide will be playing the same role for you, and, since this book is the road map that you will be following, you need to share it with your Guide before you set out on your journey.

In Chapter 3, I have included a number of characteristics to look for when choosing a Guide. After reading the list, you may feel that there is no one in your life who fits the bill. Remember, this is an idealized portrait: The perfect Guide would possess all these traits. But in the real world, you just may not know anyone who even comes close to the ideal. Don't worry. I suggest that you focus on the two or three characteristics that are most important to *you* as you try to reach *your particular goal*, and choose your Guide accordingly.

3. The willingness to go beyond your comfort zone, to drop your defenses and become vulnerable, to take a leap of faith in order to improve your life

This is the Big One. You may have set your Intention. You may have access to data about the disconnect between your current and your desired behaviors, and you may have a Guide—and even other supporters—who are ready, willing, and able to accompany you on your self-improvement journey. But if you aren't willing—deep down and for real—to make profound changes in yourself, you are not a candidate for self-coaching. You might as well close this book now and head for your comfort zone.

In self-coaching, willingness is the price of admission.

Often people think they are willing to change, but they really aren't. They may be highly motivated at the beginning, but unless they have a good deal at stake, the ardor soon cools. This is where our business coaching differs most from self-coaching. When a company retains us to coach one of its executives, the stakes tend to be high. Not going along with the coaching can raise serious questions about an executive's ability to become a high-performance player. Most of the time, people who aren't compelled to go to coaching don't have anywhere near as much at stake. They may want to prepare for a new career or get a promotion, so they decide to engage a coach. But there may not be the sense of urgency that an underperforming employee feels when coaching is "offered" by the boss.

I firmly believe that willingness is directly proportional to the amount of "skin in the game"—and that holds just as true for self-coaching as it does for being coached by another.

Take, for example, a hard-charging executive who works long hours and travels extensively. On her brief stays at home, her husband complains about the fact that she's never around for him or the kids. She feels a slight twinge of guilt but, come Sunday afternoon, she's back on another plane headed for another long week away from home.

So much for guilt! Until the next trip home, when she gets an ultimatum from her exasperated husband: things need to change, or else. . . . The ominous tone tells her that the situation is serious. Now she has real skin in the game, and she realizes that unless she's willing to pay the price, something has got to give.

Let's face it: there are payoffs and costs attached to every action we take. As long as the costs don't outweigh the payoffs, we tend to go along repeating the same behaviors. It's not until we *need* fewer costs or more payoffs that we become truly open to change. That's when we become willing for real.

Willingness also depends on how much thought we've given to what it will take to reach our Intention. It's hard enough for human beings to accept external change, and the idea of undergoing *internal* change takes a lot more getting used to. Psychologists Carlo DiClemente and James O. Prochaska have identified five distinct stages through which people progress as they attempt to change their behavior. Their Transtheoretical Model of Change[8] enumerates and explains the stages, which include:

- **Precontemplation.** Individuals in this stage are not thinking about or intending to change a problem behavior (or initiate a healthy one) in the near future (the next six months).
- **Contemplation.** An individual enters the Contemplation stage when she becomes aware of a desire to change a particular behavior (within the next six months). In this stage, individuals weigh the pros and cons of changing their behavior.
- **Preparation.** By the time individuals enter the Preparation stage, the pros in favor of attempting to change a problem behavior outweigh the cons, and action is intended in the near future (the next 30 days). Preparers often have a plan of action, but they may not be entirely committed to their plan.
- **Action.** The Action stage marks the beginning of actual behavior change. If an individual has not sufficiently prepared for change and committed to a plan of action, relapse to the problem behavior is likely.

- **Maintenance.** Individuals are said to be in the Maintenance stage when they have successfully achieved the behavior change and maintained it for at least six months. While there is still a risk of relapse, it is much less at this point.

Your degree of willingness to change your behavior depends on what stage you are in, and it would be a big mistake for you to start on this self-coaching program before you are ready. (In Chapter 1, we will go into more detail about the reasons why.) As the model demonstrates, you need to be in the Preparation stage in order to start taking action and making plans. If, after an honest self-assessment of your readiness, you find that you are still in the Contemplation or Precontemplation stage, you might not want to complete all the exercises in this book. It might be a better idea for you to read through all the chapters and get used to the idea that, when you are ready to begin, you will have all the information and tools you need to coach yourself to win.

You also might not want to embark on your self-coaching program if you are currently undergoing a major life change or an emotional upheaval. This is a demanding undertaking, and it's going to require concentrated effort. It's also going to require courage: you are going to have to face a great many truths about yourself—not all of them pleasant. You may have to listen and process feedback that's less than complimentary. You will probably experience disappointments and failures along the way. All of this makes it very risky if you aren't coming from a position of some strength. Remember, in a breakdown, it's tough to make a breakthrough.[9] It's better to wait until you are more "together."

But if you feel that there's enough at stake, if you have spent enough time contemplating the changes that you want to make, and if you are emotionally and psychologically ready to take the trip along a new pathway, then join me on this exciting journey. Together, we will be taking seven giant steps that will lead to self-discovery and self-improvement—to breakthrough performance on the job and in your life.

THE SEVEN STEPS

In the following seven chapters, I am going to take you through the "Seven Steps to Breakthrough Performance on the Job and in Your Life." At each step, I will ask you to focus on one major question. As I discuss each step, I will provide you with additional questions to guide your thinking and with tools that you can use, in real time, to find the answers that are right for you.

CHAPTER 1: CAN YOU COACH YOURSELF TO WIN?

Step 1: Determine whether or not you are self-coachable.
Ask: Am I able, ready, and willing to change my behavior permanently?

CHAPTER 2: SETTING YOUR INTENTION

Step 2: Select your Intention and commit to it.
Ask: What is my ultimate goal?

CHAPTER 3: CHOOSING YOUR TRAVELING COMPANIONS

Step 3: Identify/enroll a Guide and a Circle of Support.
Ask: Who are the people who can provide me with insight about my behavior, support, and who will be honest with me?

CHAPTER 4: WHAT'S THE MESSAGE?

Step 4: Solicit feedback.
Ask: What can these people tell me about my current behavior and how it needs to change? Or, what suggestions do you have for taking my game up to the next level?

CHAPTER 5: HOW SHOULD YOU RESPOND?

Step 5: Analyze and respond to the feedback.
Ask: What's the message that these people are giving me, and how will I respond?

CHAPTER 6: MAPPING YOUR ROUTE

Step 6: Develop your game plan.
Ask: What actions am I going to take, by when?

CHAPTER 7: GETTING AND STAYING THERE

Step 7: Track your success and recalibrate.
Ask: Am I accomplishing the goals I committed to? If not, what do I need to do to get back on track? How will I know when I have arrived?

Assessing your self-coachability—your ability to be your own coach, without engaging a professional to serve as your conscience and provide external motivation—is the first of the seven steps to breakthrough performance that we will be taking in the following chapter.

Are you ready to take that step?

CHAPTER 1

CAN YOU COACH YOURSELF TO WIN?

Determine Your Self-Coachability 1
Select and Commit to an Intention 2
Identify Your Guide and Circle of Support 3
Solicit Feedback 4
Analyze and Respond to Feedback 5
Develop and Act on a Game Plan 6
Track Your Success and Recalibrate 7
The Self-Coaching Process

If you have seen the film *Indiana Jones and the Last Crusade*, chances are that you will never forget the edge-of-the-seat scene when, in order to save his father, Indy must step off a ledge onto a bridge that he cannot see. He has to trust that it is below him and will break his fall. He literally takes a leap of faith—and lands safely.

Embarking on a program of self-improvement, whether personal or professional, means taking a figurative leap of faith: you must set your Intention, leave your comfort zone, and enter uncharted territory. What will you encounter? You might come face to face with unpleasant facts about yourself, negative feedback from others, doubts about your self-worth, feelings of inadequacy and, of course, the temptation to turn around and retreat to the tried and true. And, unlike moviedom's happy endings, in real life there's no guarantee that you'll land safely.

The willingness to take this leap of faith is essential for both successful coaching and successful *self*-coaching. If you are reading this book, I suspect that you are probably experiencing discontent with some area of your life. You may have a nagging feeling that there can be, and should be, more to life than the status quo. You are ready for change.

But change brings uncertainty. And uncertainty can be scary. Your life—and self—are bound to be different once you reach your Intention. "How different?" is the question. New doors will open and new possibilities arise. Will you be able to deal with them? Will you miss your old, familiar life and self?

This is where the leap of faith comes in. You must firmly believe that you will land safely, that the "new" will be better than the "old," that your discomfort will be temporary, and that you will feel a greater sense of fulfillment at the journey's end.

Let's do a little exploration together, just to get started. Get comfortable and take a good look inside yourself:

- What do you see and feel?
- How satisfied or happy are you with things as they are?

- Where are you professionally, emotionally, physically, and socially, especially in terms of those who matter most to you?
- Is change an option that you are willing to consider?

As you review your interior landscape, are there areas that stand out as hot spots—where you feel discomfort, unhappiness, or even pain? Don't be surprised if the hot spots that come into focus are those that you rarely bring to the surface. They may well be things that you constantly beat down, like one of those pop-up games at an arcade, or that you habitually paper over with procrastination and excuses. You may never have discussed them even with your closest friends or family.

Now, think deeper. Is there an area that, if it were changed, would represent a significant, even life-changing improvement for you?

As you engage yourself, be mindful that the act of self-reflection is not merely an intellectual exercise. You must not just *think* that the need for change is an imperative; you must also *feel* its urgency. Give it your *full* attention. And give it time. Don't expect a bolt of lightning to strike you, though be grateful if it does! As Eckhart Tolle wisely cautions:

> Some emotions are easily identified: anger, fear, grief, and so on. Others may be much harder to label. They may just be vague feelings of unease, heaviness, halfway between an emotion and a physical sensation. In any case, what matters is not whether you can attach a mental label to it but whether you can bring the feeling of it into awareness as much as possible. Attention is the key to transformation—and full attention also implies acceptance. Attention is like a beam of light—the focused power of your consciousness that transmutes everything into itself.[1]

Here, the law of parsimony should prevail. You are about to launch an important journey along a new pathway. Simplicity is a cardinal virtue for the trip! As you go through this exercise, focus on one—*and only one*—area. In my coaching experience, I have discovered that success is more likely when you don't attempt an extreme makeover of the entire landscape. (Later in the book, we will give you a few practical tools for breaking apart your areas of concern.) For now, think about one area in which your life could be significantly improved.

ARE YOU SELF-COACHABLE?

It's now decision time. Now that you have selected the area that you would like to improve, retreat once again to your private and trusted space for more reflection and deep thinking. Ask yourself

Am I *able, ready,* and *willing* to *permanently* change my *behavior*?

Concentrate on each of the five key concepts in this one question: *ability*, *readiness*, *willingness*, *permanency*, and *behavior*. Each represents an element that needs to be considered as you attempt to arrive at your answer. To guide you as you consider the question, let's take a close look at each of the five elements, one at a time.

1. It's all about behavior

For reasons that will soon become apparent, we're not going to take these elements in the order in which they appear in the question. Since any *attempt at improving yourself or your performance revolves around behavior change*, it's appropriate to begin with *behavior*, the last word in our question.

A while ago, I was asked to step in after a dispute between a male and a female executive. The male had made some remarks that were obviously sexist. The female was outraged and complained to the CEO, demanding that her male colleague be fired immediately. The CEO believed, and I concurred, that the man would be *able* to change once he became more conscious of his behavior. The female executive would hear no such talk. In her opinion, the offender was a dyed-in-the-wool misogynist—period. "Even if he changes," she said to me, "I'm not sure it will be in his bones." I explained that bones don't much matter. You can't hold someone accountable for his "bones" or his attitude; you can only hold him accountable for his behavior.

I learned very early in my executive coaching that my primary concern should be with changing behavior. That's what I'm hired for. As author and inspirational speaker Jo Berry frequently pointed out, "It's easier to act yourself into a new way of thinking than to think yourself into a new way of acting." My job is to get the people I coach to *act* differently.

When you accept a job, you also accept a package of rules related to the job. If you're a factory worker, you're probably required to "punch the clock" and take specified breaks. If you're an executive, your package comes with performance goals and "emphasis areas," which determine your compensation. From your boss's and your colleagues' vantage point, it's pretty much beside the point if every time you punch the clock, you think, "What SOBs those managers are, treating us like kindergarten kids." Or if you think your boss is the Marquis de Sade reincarnated for setting unrealistic "stretch" performance goals. As long as you meet expectations, you're free to think as you please. Your relationship with your organization is something of a "behavioral rental agreement." You agree to behave a certain way in exchange for monetary compensation.

In executive coaching, I focus on changing observable behavior, which is the only reliable indicator of performance. As your own coach, that's where your focus needs to be. Statements like "respect diversity," "be more understanding," or "be a better friend" mean nothing until you take them to a granular level of behavior. If you want to be a better family member, start by thinking about your behavior: How am I behaving? Am I doing something that causes distress? Then, ask the members of your family: "How am I doing?" and "How can I add more value to our relationship?" You might hear things like, "Don't be so impatient; listen more; give me more space to be who I am without trying to change me." These are all suggestions on which you can take action.

Getting back to the example of the "dyed-in-the-wool misogynist," I coached the man for several sessions, during which he recognized the inappropriateness of his past remarks and actions and made up his mind to behave differently in the future. Now, he and his female colleague work together effortlessly. Is he still a flaming chauvinist at heart? I don't know and, frankly, I couldn't care less. As long as he refrains from acting like one, I consider him a successful graduate of the Guttman school of coaching!

2. Are you in it for the long haul?

Sisyphus, the tragic figure of ancient Greek mythology, was condemned by the gods to push a boulder up a hill, only to have it roll back down again, so that he had to repeat the task over and over for eternity. The gods ensured that Sisyphus could not sustain the change that he so fervently sought, and many of us, Oprah included, condemn ourselves to the same fate. We spend a lifetime pursuing a goal, achieving it, falling back again, and then repeating the cycle over and over. Consciously or unconsciously, we try to game the system. We make a commitment to long-term change, but then we quietly whisper to ourselves, "This doesn't have to be forever. I'll reach my goal. Then, every so often, I'll be able to smoke a cigarette or take a drink or eat a slice of chocolate cake." Those who try to ease the pain with such self-sabotage invariably lose whatever ground they worked so hard to win.

Sustained behavioral change is the only true measure of the success of any coaching program, whether in the business or the personal realm. Unless you make up your mind that you are going to change your behavior *permanently,* you condemn yourself to forever rolling the same boulder up the same mountain.

The coaching process is first about raising our consciousness, about becoming aware of our true Intention and the barriers—both those that exist in the real world and the self-sabotaging thoughts that we hold on to—that have been keeping us from achieving that Intention.

Return to the thinking you have just done about a hot spot that you want to improve. Now, flip to Action Step 1.1 at the end of this chapter and describe what you would like to have achieved at the conclusion of this self-coaching experience.

If your answers to the questions in Action Step 1.1 indicate that you are in it for the long haul, you've passed one test for self-coachability. Now, let's go back to the central question, focusing on the third element: ability.

3. Are you *able* to change your behavior?

There are schools of psychiatry and psychology—most notably, the Freudians—that start with the premise that our behavior is "hardwired" into us as a result of either our genes or our early upbringing, or both. I don't subscribe to such theories. I couldn't work in the field of management and organization development—and I certainly couldn't be an executive coach—if I didn't have a fundamental belief that people can change. *The whole premise of executive coaching is that people are 100 percent accountable for their behavior* and that, if the stakes are high enough and they understand what their options are, *they can choose to change that behavior.*

Most people want to improve. We want to get higher-paying jobs and better performance evaluations and to engage in less destructive behavior. I don't know many people who wake up each day and say, "I think I'll screw up royally." Most of us have a deep yearning to be better coworkers or parents or partners. We want to stop spiraling downward. We have tried time and again, but it seems as though we just aren't able to do it.

In my experience, most people *do* have the ability to make changes, but either they haven't been motivated enough—they haven't had enough skin in the game—or they haven't gone about it in the right way: taking the right steps, in the right sequence, and at the right pace. If you count yourself among these people, then this book is written for you.

But even among the willing and motivated, some people are *truly unable* to make the changes needed to achieve their goals.

Something inside them keeps getting in the way; they can't help sabotaging their own efforts. When the inability to control behavior is rooted in emotional or psychological dysfunction, then coaching and self-coaching are inappropriate.

In the workplace, when we suspect that an individual whom we have been asked to coach has deep-seated psychological issues, we test this by probing her boss and her colleagues to determine if others have observed the person "acting out" or exhibiting abnormal behavior patterns. A "yes" answer suggests that it's time for either Employee Assistance or a psychiatrist or psychologist rather than an executive coach. In a moment, we will pose a number of questions designed to help you raise some red-flag issues related to whether or not you must deal with deeper issues before you can tackle self-coaching.

Another telltale sign of uncoachability is an out-of-control "inner critic." It is, of course, healthy to acknowledge our shortcomings, but when such acknowledgment leads to self-loathing and self-disgust, then the line has been crossed. People who are overly self-critical focus on their flaws and generalize from there. They label themselves: "I'm a loser. I'm stupid. I'm ugly."[2] Every mistake they make and every "bad" behavior they exhibit adds to their image of themselves as fatally flawed and beyond redemption.

Albert Ellis was the founder of Rational Emotive Behavior Therapy (REBT), which attempts to change behavior by replacing the negative, "irrational" thoughts with realistic, positive ones. He made an important distinction between a person's actions and his self-worth:

> There is no such person as *a* drunk—only a person who frequently drinks or behaves drunkenly. And no one *is* crazy—we humans only at times *behave* crazily. When we use terms like *a drunk* and *a crazy person*, we make sloppy overgeneralizations. We imply that an individual who drinks too much will *always* and *only* do so, and that a person who behaves crazily will *inevitably* behave that way. False! "Drunks" can sober up—sometimes for good. And "crazy people" can often train themselves to act less

> crazily. . . . The road to hell, as I often remind my clients, is paved with unrealistic expectations.[3]

While pursuing your Intention through this self-coaching program, you are going to have to take a cold, hard look at yourself and your current behavior. You will need to "depersonalize"—to step back and view your life *objectively*, as though you were sitting in a movie theater watching a film unfold. People who are overly critical of themselves cannot make this separation. Until they resolve the underlying problem,[4] their ego will be too closely tied to their self-perception for them to be coached or to self-coach successfully.

Flip to Action Step 1.2 at the end of this chapter, and take a few moments now to think, as honestly and objectively as you can, about your ability to coach yourself to your stated Intention. If you think that you cannot judge your ability objectively, or if you have serious doubts about your ability to do so, either seek the help of a counselor to talk the issue through or, at a minimum, ask people you trust about your behavior and whether or not they have observed anything that may indicate the presence of emotional or psychological issues that could get in the way of achieving your goal.

If you answered yes to several of the questions in Action Step 1.2, it's likely that you have some psychological issues that will prevent you from self-coaching successfully. You should probably put this book aside and come back to it when you have resolved those issues.

4. Are you *ready* to change your behavior?

We touched on the issue of readiness in the Introduction when we cited the work of DiClemente and Prochaska, who discovered that there are five stages of behavior change (Precontemplation, Contemplation, Preparation, Action, and Maintenance).[5] Their research found that it isn't until people enter the third stage, Preparation, that they are able to commit to making real changes in their life.

Why is this? DiClemente and Prochaska found that during the second stage, Contemplation, people begin to weigh the pros and cons of changing their behavior, and many of them are extremely ambivalent. This ambivalence immobilizes them, and until it is resolved, they are unable to make a commitment.

Arming a person with the facts is the best way to end this paralysis and start him moving in the right direction—i.e., into the Preparation stage, where the pros definitely outweigh the cons. One of the roles of a coach may be to educate the coachee about the negative consequences of not changing, but if you are planning to coach yourself, you are going to have to be your own educator.

It would be fairly easy for you, on your own, to calculate the pros and cons of stopping a behavior like smoking. The pros are better health, more money in your pocket, and perhaps no longer having to stand outside your office building in the rain and snow to indulge your habit. The cons are also pretty obvious: the physical discomfort of nicotine withdrawal, not having a crutch to rely on in stressful situations, and, if you have a certain image of yourself, no longer looking "cool." If you still find it hard to move out of the Contemplation stage and into the Preparation stage, you can always visit the Web site of the American Cancer Society or the American Heart Association to learn more about the ways in which cigarettes damage your body. And you can visit your doctor or a pharmacy to get information on the most effective smoking-cessation aids.

Here's a different kind of example in which information plays a central role. Let's say you are a paralegal, and you often dream of becoming a lawyer. You know the benefits: a lot less drudgery, a lot more money, and certainly more prestige. But what problems might you encounter? If you are seriously contemplating making your dream a reality, you had better get answers to the following questions:

- Do you have the aptitude to perform well on the qualifying exam?
- How long will it take you to reach your goal?

- What schools should you apply to?
- What courses do you need to take?
- Can you attend evening classes while you keep your day job?
- How much is it going to cost?
- What financial aid is available?
- How much time will you have to spend studying?

Depending on your circumstances, there may be other questions that you need to ask, such as: Will my spouse be supportive of my goal? or, How will I manage my home life? or, Will I have enough time for my friends? This is a situation in which a lot of information is required. Unless you are aware, up front, of what's going to be needed, you can't possibly make an informed decision about whether or not to go for your dream.

Remember, by the time you enter the Preparation stage, you have decided that the pros of going for your goal outweigh the cons, and you intend to take action in the near future—typically within the next 30 days.

Have you reached the Preparation stage? Flip to Action Step 1.3 at the end of this chapter to be certain. If your answer to the final question, "Are you convinced that you have a lot more to gain than to lose by going for your goal?" is yes, you are probably a good candidate for self-coaching, but you still have one question to answer, and it's The Big One.

5. Are you *willing* to change your behavior?

If you've come this far with me, you have probably already answered, "Yes, I am willing to change my behavior." But there's a second question that follows naturally from the first, and that I'm going to ask you now:

Are you willing to do whatever is necessary to change your behavior?

That's a tough question, and it requires a lot more soul-searching. To answer it, you need to know, specifically, what's going to be asked of you during the self-coaching process. If only you could just snap your fingers and, presto, begin behaving differently. But reality doesn't work that way, and maybe that's for the better. Being in a hurry often means that you're not *in thought*, which is a key to successful self-change.

Here are a few of the things that you must be willing to do to change your behavior:

- **Acknowledge the fact that you, and only you, are responsible for your failure to achieve your goals**. A few years ago, we worked with the senior team of a large pharmaceutical company. Licensing was central to the company's growth strategy, but the head of business development and licensing just didn't seem to be able to bring in licensed products to supplement the company's own offerings. The rest of the team repeatedly tried to find out why his efforts were not succeeding and to coach him to success. His response to questions about his effectiveness was always that others weren't giving him the support he needed, were not focused on the right areas, didn't provide the right analyses, and on and on. After a while, it became apparent that this executive was never going to acknowledge the part *he* was playing in failing to meet his goals, and he was terminated.

  People do the same thing in their personal life: they attempt to shift the blame for their problems and failures to others. These people come from a *victim place*, and when they tell me that bad things just happen to them or that other people are the cause of their problems, I don't buy it.

  A good friend of mine teaches physical education in a high school in New Jersey. He recently told me that he has been having problems with several of the other teachers: they had complained to the administration that he was violating safety rules, failing to put equipment away after his classes, keeping students in the gym after the bell had rung, and so on. According to him, they were "ratting on him" and were "out to get him." My response to him was to ask, *"What part do you play in that?"* He was quite surprised by the question, and he actually got angry. But I continued, saying, "I'm telling you that you play a role in that. Don't expect me to believe that you are just there, a good guy to whom bad things happen. How do you show up to these people as someone who presents an inviting back for them to stick a knife in? How do you do that?"

Of course, my friend continued to insist that I was wrong, that he had no part in what was happening to him. But I wasn't wrong. These people chose to treat him a certain way, and it was because he sent them, consciously or unconsciously, an invitation to do it. My friend is a wonderful guy, but he's not willing to acknowledge that, whatever is going on in his life, he is a willing co-conspirator.

All of us have a hand in writing our life's script, whether we are conscious of it or not. Effective coaching raises your consciousness. When you are conscious of being accountable, you realize that you are the one who is creating your story.

- **In order for your self-coaching to work, you cannot be a victim.** You must be willing to say, and mean, "I am responsible for my outcomes."
- **Go beyond acknowledgment—to action.** Some people are what I call "responsible victims": they acknowledge the part they play in creating a situation that isn't working for them—they don't have the right job or the right relationships, they haven't lost the weight they need to, they aren't living where they want to, and so on. But they stop there; they own up to their faults over and over again, but they never make the needed changes.

Let me repeat: Coaching is about changing behavior. *Becoming conscious is merely an academic exercise if it's not accompanied by the willingness to take action.*

- **Drop your defenses.** When someone questions or criticizes us, our first reaction is to defend ourselves against the attack or to flee, often by going underground. We perceive any criticism or questioning as a personal attack that we have to fight off or flee from.
- **To succeed at self-coaching, view feedback not as a threat, but as a gift.** One executive with whom we worked took this advice quite literally. He told his staff that if they saw him not living up to his commitments and came to him with that feedback, he would view it as a gift. Then he went to Starbucks and bought a number of gift cards, which he distributed to his staff, instructing them to give one back to him, with their feedback, each time he transgressed, so that they too would feel as if they were giving him a gift.
- **Depersonalization is another key to becoming less defensive.** I tell the executives I coach that they need to view their colleagues' critiques of them purely as a "business case." It's their *performance* that is being discussed, not their worth as a human being.

  Think about the way you tend to react when someone gives you negative feedback: Do you feel belittled or minimized? Does your blood pressure rise? Is your first thought to "get even" rather than to get it right?

  As you move through the self-coaching process, you may hear some uncomplimentary things about yourself from others. You are also going to have to look at yourself with a critical eye—the way you might look at the packaging on a box—and not feel emotionally invested.

Unless you are willing to drop your defenses, self-coaching is not an option.

- **Reframe your "stories."** I was once asked to coach a leader who saw conflict within his team as a bad thing. To his mind, if there was any discord on the team, it meant that something wasn't working right. So, any time people started to challenge one another, he stepped in and shut down the conversation.

  This executive had a "story" about disagreement of any kind or magnitude: "It's a bad thing; the organization will suffer negative consequences if it is permitted." When I first began working with him, he wasn't even aware that he had a story: *a preconceived notion he was holding on to that affected the way he viewed reality.* I pointed out that my colleagues and I were there to help him develop a high-performing leadership team, and that one of the attributes of a high-performing team is the ability to bring conflict out into the open and handle it honestly, candidly, and in a depersonalized way. Squelching honest differences of opinion was the last thing he should be doing if he wanted better results from his team.

  As we talked, it became clear that he was extremely fearful of what would happen if open discord was allowed. He really believed that the senior team would begin to unravel, to actually turn into battling Hatfields and McCoys. He was especially afraid that *he* would lose control of the team completely.

  As he became conscious of his story, he began to realize where it emanated from. He had been brought up in a family that was very repressed. Issues between family members were always handled behind closed doors. When he first joined this company, it was very hierarchical, and the "closed-door approach" was exactly the way management preferred to handle discord. The behavior pattern he had followed all his life worked perfectly in that environment. Then our firm was brought in to create a different organizational model, one that worked horizontally and transparently. He was struggling mightily with the new way of interacting because it was counter to everything he had been raised to believe.

Stories can exert near-tyrannical force on your behavior. In the case of this conflict-shy executive, he clearly was up against his comfort zone. When we began exploring the issues, he, in effect, was saying, "I have a story. I have a box around what works for me. I don't want to go outside that box because I am afraid—I anticipate future pain, and I want to avoid it."

Eventually, through coaching and the acquisition of conflict management skills, he was able to overcome his fear. He was able to reframe his story to say, "Conflict does not have to be destructive. If it is managed properly, it can be a positive force. By learning how to manage conflict, my team and I will benefit."

We all have stories about why we can't or shouldn't make changes in our life:

"I can't quit smoking; I'll gain weight."

"I'll never be able to get a promotion; I'm not one of the 'in' group."

"I can't get my own apartment; my mother depends on me."

"I can't go back to college; it's too expensive."

"I can't stand up to my husband; he's got a violent temper."

"I can't ask the boss for a raise; he'll turn me down and probably fire me as well."

Albert Ellis termed these stories "Irrational Beliefs" and felt that they are the underlying cause of many of our emotional problems. Here's how he said Rational Emotive Behavior Therapy helps resolve the problems caused by these beliefs:

> Whatever your emotional upsets are, REBT shows you how to find the thoughts that underlie them—and thereby succeed in deciphering the "unconscious" messages you

> transmit to yourself. Once you begin to see, understand, and begin to Dispute the Irrational Beliefs that go with your unhealthy feelings, you make yourself aware of your "unconscious" thoughts and greatly enhance your power to change them and reduce your disturbances.[6]

In the same way, becoming conscious of the stories that you tell yourself, then disputing and reframing them, can greatly enhance your power to change your behavior and achieve your goals.

Unless you are willing to reframe your stories, you will never get "unstuck" from your current situation.

- **Go public.** Business coaching can never be done in a vacuum. There are always a certain number of people, besides the coach and the coachee, who must be involved in the process. A direct supervisor or an HR professional must serve as both a mentor to the coachee and a liaison with the chosen coach. Colleagues must observe and comment on behavior before, during, and after the coaching. Enlisting a well-chosen mentor and group of stakeholders is essential for success in business coaching.

  In fact, it is essential in *all* coaching, including self-coaching. That is why we are going to ask you to choose a personal "Guide" (the equivalent of a mentor in business coaching) and a "Circle of Support" (the equivalent of stakeholders), who will serve as your extended self and be there to provide counsel and support if and when the going gets rough. These people will be committed to helping you succeed. They will also hold you accountable for behaving in accordance with your stated Intention.

  Many self-help books are meant to be read and followed in private. They ask you to be introspective, to look inside yourself to uncover your problems and arrive at solutions. This book takes a different approach. We are going to ask you to identify and enlist supporters who will help you set your Intention, develop your Game Plan, and keep you honest. If you've ever tried to coach yourself without the help of others, you'll be surprised at how much easier it is to reach your Intention when you have supporters by your side.

The willingness to enlist the support of others, being totally frank with them, and accepting their honest feedback is an important precondition for successful self-coaching.

IT'S TIME TO DECIDE

Now that you've read through this chapter and considered the questions we've put to you, you've probably got a pretty good idea of whether or not you are going to be able to coach yourself successfully. Before you make your final decision, we suggest that you revisit some of our earlier questions and answer several others in Action Step 1.4 at the end of this chapter.

If your answers indicate that you are going to be able to coach yourself successfully, you are now ready to take Step 2, "Setting Your Intention." That's what we'll be doing in Chapter 2.

Action Step 1.1: Are You in It for the Long Haul?

Which type of behavior change would you like to achieve? Think of Intentions along the lines of the following as you answer the questions that follow:

- *Stopping an undesirable or harmful behavior: overeating, smoking, drinking to excess, treating others badly, avoiding responsibility*
- *Becoming better at an existing skill or learning a new one—for your job, a sport, a personal relationship*
- *Accomplishing a very specific goal: making a career change, running a marathon, getting a promotion, getting a better job, meeting the right partner*

On a separate sheet of paper or on our Web site, answer the following questions:

1. Describe your Intention as specifically as possible. What would a successful outcome look like for you?
2. Have you ever tried to achieve this particular Intention before? How many times did you try? Were you ever completely successful? For how long?
3. If you never reached your Intention, why do you think you derailed?
4. If you did reach your goal, but weren't able to sustain your success, what caused you to slip back?
5. If you understand the factors that caused you to slip back in the past, do you think you will be able to address them this time around? Answer yes, no, or don't know.
6. Look back at your previous attempts and be completely honest with yourself. Were you committed to making permanent changes in your life, or did you believe that after a while you

could go back to your old behavior? If you thought that the change didn't need to be permanent, why?

7. If you intend to reach this Intention again, with the help of this self-coaching program, are you prepared to put aside these self-sabotaging thoughts this time around? If so, how?

There's one additional question that you should ask before you commit to an Intention, and it's a deceptively simple one: Is it your *Intention? Are you doing this because* you *want to, or because someone else is asking—or demanding—it of you?*

Are you responding to an ultimatum from someone else: "change or I'm out of here" from a spouse or partner; "change or you're out of here" from the boss? This doesn't mean that your efforts won't be successful—after all, you're bound to be highly motivated when the stakes are so high. But there's a red flag here. It tells me that you may not be totally committed to permanent *behavior change.*

How many people start dating someone who hates smoking, so they give it up—until they break up with that person and meet another, more tolerant mate? I've known executives who managed to change their behavior while they were under the watchful eye of the boss who recommended that they go through coaching. When they changed bosses, it didn't take long for their old behaviors to reemerge.

You are always at greater risk of relapse when you don't "own" your Intention.

8. Are you certain that this is *your* Intention and that you are not trying to please someone else? If that person were no longer in the picture, would you still be willing to commit permanently to this Intention?

Answer yes or no to these questions. If you cannot honestly say yes to both, you may want to do some more thinking before making a commitment. I suggest that you read more of this book in order to get a better idea of what lies ahead before completing the rest of the Action Steps.

Action Step 1.2: Are You Able to Change Your Behavior?

On a sheet of paper or on our Web site, respond to each of the following questions regarding your ability to evaluate your behavior objectively and make adjustments as needed; use the goal that you defined in Action Step 1.1. To determine whether or not you have cause for concern, ask yourself:

1. Have you tried to reach this or other Intentions in the past and been unable to stop yourself from sabotaging your own efforts? Answer yes or no.
2. Are you ever unable to control your words and actions? (For example, do you become physically or verbally abusive to others? After the fact, do you often regret what you have said or done?) If so, detail your experiences.
3. Do you sometimes find it difficult to understand or explain why you have acted in a certain way? If yes, why do you think this is so?
4. Do you think of yourself as worthless or a total failure? Answer yes or no.
5. Do you think or speak about yourself in general terms: "I'm a drunk/an abuser/stupid/lazy/incompetent/unlovable/rotten through and through"? Answer yes or no.

Action Step 1.3: Are You Ready to Change Your Behavior?

On a sheet of paper or on our Web site, answer the following questions:

1. Think about the Intention that you set for yourself at the beginning of this chapter. What benefits would you get from achieving it?
2. What difficulties or problems might you have to face (i.e., what price would you have to pay in terms of money, time, expenditure of energy, emotional upheaval, effect on your relationships, amount of discomfort, and so on) in order to achieve this Intention?

3. Are you convinced that you have a *lot more* to gain than to lose by going for your goal? Answer yes or no.

Action Step 1.4: Are You Self-Coachable?

To decide, on a separate sheet of paper or on our Web site, answer yes, no, or not sure to each of the following questions:

- *Do you see the benefits of changing your* behavior?
  1. *Do you have a burning desire to improve your life; to be a better employee, colleague, friend, or family member; to raise your performance in a certain area; or to rid yourself of undesirable behaviors?*
  2. *Can you clearly envision what a "happy ending" would look like? (How would you show up differently if you realized your Intention? How would your life be better?)*
  3. *Are you willing to acknowledge that there are areas within yourself that you need to change/improve?*
- *Are you willing to change your behavior* permanently?
  4. *If you have realized your Intention before but weren't able to maintain your success, do you know what caused you to backslide?*
  5. *Are you willing to take the necessary actions to keep these things from causing you to derail this time around?*
  6 *Are you committed to changing your behavior* permanently *this time around?*
  7. *Are you changing for yourself and not to please someone else?*
- *Do you have the* ability *to change?*
  8. *Are you psychologically secure enough to "look into the mirror" at an unvarnished image of yourself?*
  9. *Are you able to step back and take a depersonalized look at yourself and your situation? (For example, can you make an objective but not overly critical evaluation of your behavior?)*

10. *Do you feel that you are in control of your emotions and behavior?*
11. *Are you able to listen to critiques from others without getting angry, lashing back, or quickly dismissing the criticisms as untrue?*
12. *Are you sure that you do not have any unresolved psychological issues that you need to deal with before you embark on a self-coaching program?*

- *Are you* ready *to change?*

13. *Are you focused on the future?*
14. *Does your inner dialogue revolve around your Intention and how to make it happen (rather than continually debating with yourself the need to do so)?*
15. *Do you clearly see the payoffs from change and the costs of not changing?*
16. *Are you convinced that you have significantly more to gain than to lose by going for your Intention?*

- *Are you* willing *to change?*

17. *Do you acknowledge the fact that you, and only you, are responsible for your failure to achieve your goals?*
18. *Can you rise above needing to look good, be in control, and so on, as you work on changing?*
19. *Are you willing to let go of stories that you have been telling yourself to explain your problems or shift the blame?*
20. *Are you willing to enlist a support group to help you achieve your Intention?*
21. *Are you willing to be totally frank with your support group?*
22. *Are you willing to accept your support group's honest feedback and not be defensive or resentful?*

Here is information to help you interpret your answers:

Questions 1–3. *No and not sure answers in this area indicate the lack of a real incentive to change. It's likely that your efforts will fail because you aren't convinced that you need to change in the first place.*

Questions 4–7. *If you didn't answer yes to all four questions, you may be able to achieve your Intention, but it's highly unlikely that your success will be long-lasting.*

Questions 8–12. *No and not sure answers here are an indication that you need to do some work in other areas, perhaps with professional help, before you attempt to self-coach.*

Questions 13–16. *If you couldn't answer yes to these questions, you probably need to take more time to prepare yourself for the process of self-coaching. Think about the costs and payoffs, do some research, then come back and revisit this chapter.*

Questions 17–22. *Remember, willingness is a must. If you weren't able to answer yes to all of the questions in this section, you will probably find excuses and engage in self-sabotage, preventing your self-coaching efforts from ending in success.*

CHAPTER 2

SETTING YOUR INTENTION

Determine Your Self-Coachability
1
Select and Commit to an Intention
2
Identify Your Guide and Circle of Support
3
Solicit Feedback
4
Analyze and Respond to Feedback
5
Develop and Act on a Game Plan
6
Track Your Success and Recalibrate
7
The Self-Coaching Process

When you are diagnosed with a terminal disease:

> . . . it takes a while to get past the surrealism, to really get it that your time may be limited, and that how you are spending your time right now is how you are choosing to spend what is left of your life. . . . It finally hit me that holding on to my typical patterns wasn't going to do anything but burn me out and cause me to fade away with no additional contribution to myself or anyone else. It was time to face the fact that my life has changed dramatically, and I either needed to redefine myself or let the illness do it for me.
>
> Once I got it that things had to change, I started to shift my priorities. My work was no longer being a management consultant. My work was now to demonstrate how to take responsibility for my own survival and live with intention to find a way to beat an unbeatable disease.[1]

The author of these words set his Intention to beat the unbeatable. And when he did, he took control of his illness and his life.

In 2000, at the age of 50, Joe Wions was one of our firm's most valued consultants, and he loved his work. He and his wife, Diane, were the proud parents of two young adults, ages 17 and 20. He worked out at a gym three to five times a week, and he enjoyed tennis, skiing, backpacking, hiking, and softball. He planted trees and shrubs and grew his own vegetables. The world, it seemed, was Joe's.

Then Joe began to experience weakness in his right leg. Three years later, after myriad tests and procedures, he was officially diagnosed with ALS, commonly known as Lou Gehrig's disease. A progressive neurodegenerative disease that affects nerve cells in the brain and the spinal cord, ALS eventually leads to paralysis and death.

Joe's initial reactions were many and typical: worry about his family's financial security, distress about the pain they were going to have to endure, anger and sadness at the thought that he would never know his grandchildren, regret for all the things he hadn't done, and, of course, fear of the pain and increasing disability that lay ahead.

But Joe chose not to become a victim. He set an *Intention* to fight back with everything he had. And since his diagnosis seven years ago, that Intention has guided his every action. He has spent every day reaffirming, in words and actions, his Intention to beat this disease. His life is a study in discipline, dedicated to Intention-focused action: conducting research on the Internet; flying to Europe for special treatments; trying new diets, vitamin supplements, chelation, and other body-cleansing programs; learning meditation and mind-control techniques; and maintaining strong relationships with his family, his friends, his former colleagues, and his community. He has attracted a large group of caring individuals—he refers to them as his army of angels—who are always there for him, with physical, financial, and emotional support.

Despite great physical limitations (he is dependent on a machine to support his breathing), Joe has just finished writing a book on his experience. Ten years after contracting ALS and seven years after receiving a formal diagnosis, he is one of the most alive, intellectually vital, and socially connected people I know. Joe Wions is living proof of what a human being can accomplish by setting a true Intention and never wavering from it.

INTENTION DEFINED

"Intention," the ancient Greek philosopher Aristotle wrote long before there was a Wayne Dyer or even a Sigmund Freud, "is a deliberate desire of things which are in our power to bring about." He viewed Intention as unique; it is meant for action.[2] Borrowing from Aristotle's insight, Intention has five key qualities:

- Setting an Intention takes deliberation. You've got to think about it.
- Intentions must be realistic. You must be able to bring them about.

- Intentions state *what you have decided to do*. They are charged with commitment.
- Intentions are about *choosing your future* (Aristotle's word for Intention, *proaireton*, literally means "to choose before").[3] Intentions are about action. You set them in order to make a change.
- Intentions are about action. You set them in order to make a change.

Intentions can move mountains, or at least nations. Recall a few of the famous Intentions that have changed history:

- *Liberté, égalité, fraternité*—the French Revolution
- Life, liberty, and the pursuit of happiness—the American Declaration of Independence
- Bread, land, and peace—the Russian Revolution
- "You ask what is our aim? . . . It is victory."
  —Winston Churchill
- "Today we have Germany, tomorrow the world.
  —Adolf Hitler
- Swords into Ploughshares—the motto of the United Nations

Whether for good or evil, Intentions have a way of focusing people, galvanizing their energy, and prompting them to take action. They are a force not only for large-scale social and political change, but for personal change as well. It is unlikely that you will win a Nobel Prize, find a cure for cancer, bring home Olympic Gold, occupy the Oval Office, win the Teacher-of-the-Year Award, or rise to the top of your organization without setting an Intention to excel and then living by and up to that Intention.

Intentions need not be extraordinary. Setting them and then acting to bring them about can and should be built into the warp and woof of everyday life. You may wake up on a cold winter's morning, look out at the falling snow, and think, "I intend to drive very carefully this morning to avoid an accident." You may stop at the supermarket on the way home and say, "I'm through grazing for snacks and sweets; I intend to buy only healthy food." Or you may set an Intention to substitute lunchtime power walks for sitting around eating club sandwiches and gossiping with colleagues. Your Intention may not move nations or even change the course of your personal history. But who cares? It's your Intention, and because it makes a difference to you, it has inherent validity.

All Intentions—individual or large-scale, honorable or misguided, realistic or a stretch—share a common trait: *they are about being conscious*—first, of the end state that you want to achieve; then of the choices that you'll need to make to get there; and finally, of the choices you've been making that have kept you from achieving this state. Consciousness of our Intentions enables us to command our future.

When you set an Intention and are serious about it, you cordon off a "no-trespassing" zone for any action or decision that might get in the way of your desired state. If you truly want to become a great author, you'll opt for spending more time writing at your computer than sitting on the couch watching television. If you want to commit to stop drinking, you'll avoid the route that passes your favorite bar. If you sincerely want to have a better relationship with your children, you're going to spend more time listening and less time lecturing. All these changes require new levels of consciousness and commitment.

One of the most popular books on Intention is Dr. Wayne Dyer's *The Power of Intention*, which was published in 2004 and later formed the basis of a PBS television special. Dyer's work is based on his belief that there is an energy, or force, in the universe that we can tap into in order to better our lives and manifest our deepest desires. In his mind, he says, "Intention is now something much greater than a determined ego or individual will. . . . [It is] a force that we all have within us . . . a field of energy that flows invisibly beyond the reach of our normal, everyday habitual patterns. It's there even before our actual conception."[4]

For those who are interested in exploring the spiritual nature of Intention, Dyer's book is an excellent place to start. It offers compelling examples of people who have realized their dreams by putting their faith in, and becoming receptive to, this universal force. Aristotle's notion of Intention offers a different pathway. It doesn't require that you believe in an outside force to help you achieve your goals. To Aristotle, the starting point of all change is *you*. You are the force.

If you prefer to think of "you" in terms of a larger energy force, by all means do so. But if plugging into such a force isn't your thing, there's no need to worry. Think of yourself as an *ens completum* (an end unto yourself), and forge ahead to create your own "happy ending."

THE POWER OF PASSION

If you've taken the questions in Chapter 1 seriously, then you have a happy ending within your grasp. Stay with that sought-after result. It will be the focus of your self-coaching as you follow the program outlined in this book.

For your self-coaching to work, being passionate about the desired result is a cardinal virtue. We often set goals for ourselves, such as improving our job performance or career prospects, losing weight, going back to college, reworking our résumé, engaging in regular exercise, and so on. But we do so by trying to impose mind over matter, without engaging our emotions and our heart, which is why time after time we fail to achieve our goals. I believe it was the French mathematician and philosopher Blaise Pascal who stated, "The mind says one thing, the heart says another, and it's the heart that usually prevails." When I speak of setting an Intention, I'm first and foremost talking about locking into an end result that ignites your passion. Deep down, the happy ending you envision should be nothing less than a must, a gotta have, a categorical imperative. Such depth of passion regarding your Intention charges you up for success.

Setting your Intention requires passion and heart, but it also requires a deep, lasting commitment and a sound process.

THE PROCESS

The Intention-Setting Process

- Write down your Intention.
- Declare your Intention to others.
- Begin living in your Intention.
- Uncover your "stories."
- Reevaluate your stories.
- Weigh the payoffs and costs.
- Create new stories.

The First Step in the Process Is to Write Down Your Intention

In Chapter 1, we asked you to do some serious soul-searching and focus on a change that significantly improves your life. Now it's time to connect that thinking to an Intention. Flip to Action Step 2.1 at the end of this chapter to start developing your Intention.

Next, Declare Your Intention to Others

This is where our self-coaching program differs from many others. I have said it already, but it bears repeating: *you cannot coach yourself in a vacuum.*

I say this for two reasons. First, going on record with your Intention increases the probability that you will follow through. It gives voice to your commitment and keeps you honest. When I'm explaining this step, I'm often asked, "Doesn't this put you under a lot of pressure?" My answer is, "It depends on your story." If your story is, "If other people know about my Intention, I'll be embarrassed if I fail," it's a clear indication that your Intention isn't very strong. Doubt corrupts the will to succeed. If, on the other hand, you view "going public" not as a source of pressure, but as a means of gaining support, that's indicative of a pretty strong Intention, which is less likely to get derailed.

The second reason for declaring your Intention is to start making things happen. Quite often, going public brings unexpected positive consequences. Wayne Dyer cites several examples to prove his point that if you have an Intention, and if you are open to receiving help from the universe, help will begin to come.[5] Werner Erhard, founder of est, has a similar point of view, which is expressed in the relationship that he sees between "context" and "content." Once you create a "context" for your life (i.e., an Intention), Erhard maintains, it will attract the "content" (i.e., the actions or help) that you need to achieve that Intention.[6]

I personally can attest to the fact that on several occasions, help came to me almost immediately when I declared my Intention *to other people*.

As a child, I loved physical activity: swimming, running, biking, sports of all kinds. That love carried over into my adult life, and I still enjoy "playing." Unfortunately, my busy schedule and the amount of travel that I do make it very difficult for me to follow a consistent workout routine. I manage to work out with a personal trainer on Saturdays but, during the week, it's difficult for me to stick to a fitness regime.

A while ago, I began thinking about what I did to keep in shape during my senior year in college. Between carrying a full academic load, student-teaching, and a long daily commute, my schedule was grueling. I hit on the idea of doing 50 push-ups every morning, before I left the house, as the best way of staying fit and strong in the least amount of time. What if I were to set that Intention again?

At first, the idea of doing the same number of push-ups at age 58 that I did at age 20 was totally daunting. I censored the thought and told myself to get real and quit dreaming about it. But the challenge began to intrigue me: how cool would it be if, at 58, I could accomplish that goal? I decided to set that Intention and declare it. I told my trainer, my wife, my friends, several of my colleagues, and even a few clients.

No sooner did I do so than my trainer found ways to integrate push-ups into my weekly routine, colleagues referred me to articles on push-ups in fitness magazines, and clients started giving me tips and sharing their personal techniques for push-ups. Did the universe hear my Intention and respond with all this support? Dyer would say that it did; Erhard would say that I created my context, and it attracted the necessary content. All I can say is that the people to whom I declared my Intention heard it and rallied around me. Professing brings out your allies. Flip to Action Step 2.2 at the end of the chapter and create a list of the people to whom you will declare your intention.

P.S.: It took me two months to work up to it, but I am now able to do 50 push-ups with no problem. No matter how late I get in or how early I get up, whether I feel terrific or under the weather, I do between 50 and 100 push-ups every morning. It has become the living, breathing manifestation of my Intention.

Begin Living in Your Intention

Up to this point, you've been doing some serious thinking about your life situation and your Intention. Now it's time for some fun. Let's leave reality and enter the realm of imagination.

Imagine that you are watching a film. You are the star, and the film is about your life. Not your life as it has been up to this point, but your life after you have turned your Intention into reality. Such end-point thinking is more than fun. It draws the future into your present behavior. Hockey great Bobby Orr once said that he could see the puck go into the net before he took a shot. And track legend

Jackie Joyner-Kersee said that at the starting line, she already envisioned herself winning the race. You create the future by "seeing" it in the present.

Let's say that your Intention is to be seen as a leader in your industry. Pretend that you have been transformed from a little-known executive to CEO of the Year. Perhaps you have been asked to deliver a speech at a major industry conference. Maybe you are being interviewed by the *Wall Street Journal*. Or maybe you've been invited to hold forth at a White House private briefing. Allow your imagination free rein as you fill in as many details of the situation as you can.

Don't just look at the images; try to capture the feelings you are experiencing in each scene:

- Where are you?
- How are you dressed?
- How is your hair cut?
- How do you carry yourself?
- What are you feeling?
- Who is around you?
- What messages are you conveying?
- How does your voice sound?
- How are people reacting to you?

The more often you watch the movie in your head, the more real it becomes, until it does, in fact, seem as though it already exists. When, in your mind, the future state becomes doable, you've completed one more step toward setting your Intention.

The beauty of this "movie-making" exercise is that it works just as well for any Intention. If you want to lose 30 pounds in six months, begin envisioning

- What you look like when you are 30 pounds lighter
- What your social life is like

- Where you shop; what size clothes you buy; how they fit
- How you look in a swimsuit
- How you feel when you look in the mirror

I routinely conduct this exercise with my coaching clients. Recently, Steve, a human resources executive in a Fortune 100 company, had just been promoted to head of HR for the Asia/Pacific Region, and the company's COO recommended that I coach him through the transition period. The COO wasn't worried about Steve's ability to handle his new responsibilities, but he was concerned about the way people outside the department viewed him. One major problem: because of Steve's low-key, nonassertive personality, his internal clients perceived him as being not highly engaged in their issues, indecisive, conflict-averse, and without any real power in the company.

I began by asking Steve what his Intention was. What would the happy ending look like if our coaching sessions were successful? His answer: he would be seen not just as a hiring-and-firing manager, but as a strong person whom others would rely on to provide them with the talent they needed and whom they would seek out for advice and counsel on all matters relating to human resources.

I asked him to project forward to that end state. In a meeting, what was his new persona doing? How was he interacting with others? How did he comport himself? When interfacing with a colleague one on one, how did he open the meeting? What mood was he projecting? How well was he listening? What was his body language like? Did his demeanor change in social situations?

His answers to these questions enabled us to set a very specific Intention and to develop a plan to realize it. Since our initial meeting, he has been working on replacing his old behaviors with the ones he envisioned: saying more in cross-functional meetings, volunteering for projects outside his own area of expertise, and offering more information. At the end of each encounter with an internal client, he makes sure that he and the client "contract" for expectations, next steps, time frames, and responsibilities. In staff meetings, he solicits the opinions of his department members, asking: What issues are of concern to you? What resources do you need? What help can I give you?

And it's working. His confidence has risen dramatically, and feedback from his coworkers indicates that they too are confident that his promotion was well deserved. By living in his Intention, this executive brought his Intention to life.

Uncover Your "Stories"

Now that you're fired up and passionate about your happy ending, you undoubtedly want to move quickly into action.

Whoa! Not so fast. Between the promise and the fulfillment lies some rocky terrain that must first be traveled. You must now take a hard look at your "going-in stories": the beliefs that you hold, consciously or subconsciously, about your ability to manifest your Intention in reality. Going-in stories act as a kind of undertow on our behavior, exercising a powerful, often-hidden pull on how we perceive reality, make decisions, and act.

As we mentioned in Chapter 1, Albert Ellis was the father of Rational Emotive Behavior Therapy (REBT). Back in 1955, he introduced his now widely accepted system, which aimed to change people's behavior by changing the way they view reality. Ellis maintained, and I agree, that people have far more choices than they realize and that many of the limitations that keep us from achieving happiness are self-imposed:

> Much of [people's] "conditioning" actually consists of self-conditioning. Therefore, a therapist, a teacher, or *even a book* [my italics] can help them to see healthy alternatives and to choose to reeducate and retrain themselves so that they reduce their self-created emotional difficulties. Consequently, REBT keeps developing many educative methods to show people how they behave self-defeatingly and how they can inspire themselves to change.[7]

The goal of Ellis's therapy was to get people to become aware of the Irrational Beliefs that they were holding on to, then replace them with "Rational Beliefs" that would enable them to begin taking control of their life.

One of Ellis's major contributions to the field of psychology was his "ABC Model." The model makes the point that the emotional Consequences (C) that we experience after Activating Experiences (A) are not the direct result of the experiences themselves. Our reactions are the result of the Belief System (B) that we hold. When our Belief System is made up of Rational Beliefs, the emotional Consequences are positive and healthy. When we hold Irrational Beliefs, the Consequences are unhealthy, negative emotions.

Let me paraphrase an example that Ellis gives to illustrate the model:

> A man is preparing to go on a job interview. If he has Rational Beliefs, he may say to himself before the interview, "I want this job, so I've got to go through this interview. I'm dreading it, but if I don't face it, I won't get the job. Maybe I won't get it anyway, but I've got to at least try." This man creates healthy Consequences for himself based on these Rational Beliefs. Even the negative emotions he feels, such as the anticipation that he might not get the job, are healthy ones.
>
> Another man is also anticipating a job interview. But his Irrational Beliefs direct his inner voice to say, "What if I go to the interview and don't get the job, or if I get the job and then prove to be incompetent? That would be awful. I would be a worm!" The resulting emotional Consequences of these Beliefs are unhealthy and damaging.[8]

What I call "going-in stories" or "core limiting beliefs" are the equivalent of Ellis's Irrational Beliefs, and many of the coaching sessions I lead are directed toward making people conscious, often for the first time in their life, of these preconceived notions and the powerful negative effect they have on behavior—specifically, the way in which they keep us from making positive changes in our life.

We often create unhealthy, negative emotions by imposing our irrational beliefs, or going-in stories, on neutral events that occur in our life. In the office, the boss walks by without a nod or a smile. At home, your spouse seems preoccupied and not interested in hearing about your day. Looked at objectively, these events are data points. They are occurrences that take place "out there" in social space. But, when you have a going-in story, you look at such events or experiences through a tinted lens. The boss passed you by without recognizing your existence; she must be displeased with you—in fact, she's probably heading to her office to prepare your pink slip. You must be the cause of your husband's inattentiveness; what did you do wrong? In each case, your response is colored by emotion, by the conversations you are having with yourself about what transpired. Figure 2.1 depicts what happens when we subjectivize objective reality.

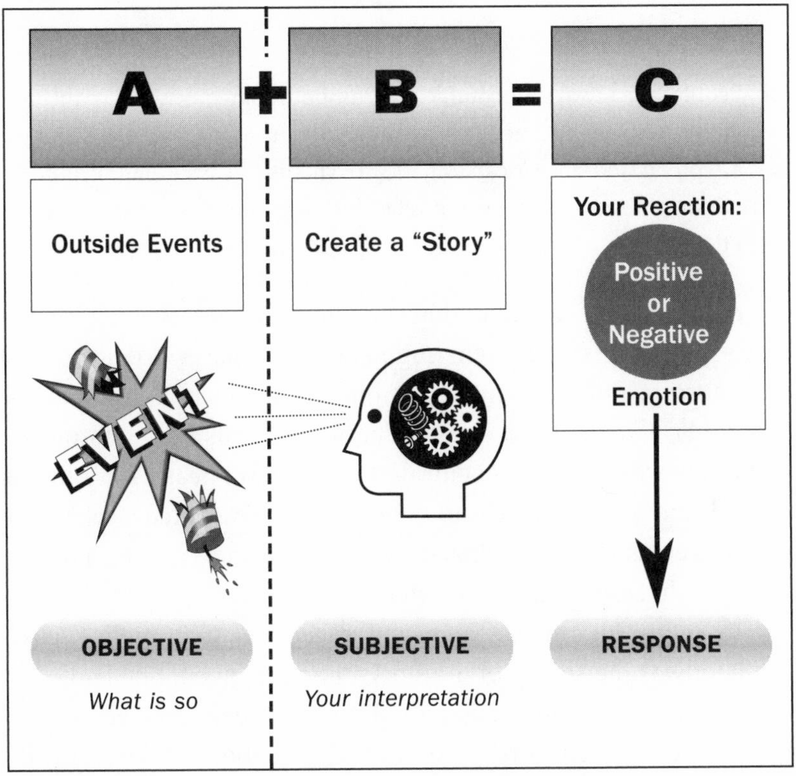

FIGURE 2.1 We Respond to Our Stories Instead of to Reality

Our going-in stories come from many sources. How we react to a situation depends in large part on our past experience in the same or similar situations. Past events, especially high-impact ones, occur and are forever engraved on our memory, where they create present expectations. Sometimes this is a good thing: the child who experiences a finger-on-a-hot-stove episode is unlikely to get burned again. But it can also hold us back: "I told my last boss the truth one too many times, and he fired me. I'm going to keep my mouth shut in my new job."

I remember coaching the executive vice president of a personal care company who happened to be a person of color. After the turnover in her division began to rise, I was asked to work with her to improve her interpersonal skills. She was viewed as a model of efficiency who was disconnected emotionally. When I suggested that she try to show a more people-friendly side, she countered with her story:

> People are always uncomfortable around someone who is different from them. They feel disconnected from me because I am a woman and an African American. This is always going to put me at a disadvantage in the relationship game, no matter what I do.

A rich source of nonrational going-in stories is what sociologists term the *implicit* environment. It's what we deduce and then absorb, often as children, from the interactions around us. When her parents argue and that argument boils over into rage, a child may well develop a better-to-be-seen-than-heard story that is carried into adulthood. Or an older brother, frustrated because he did not get his way, may whack a younger sibling, creating a might-makes-right story in the youngster.

To return to the disconnected executive, her implicit environment was the source of the story I just described. She had often overheard her parents talking around the kitchen table about how whites were uncomfortable around blacks and treated them differently. Her "story" was many years in the making. My response to her was, "Your story about your colleagues is that race plays a role in your relationship with them, and that's a story you need to let go of."

The *explicit* environment—messages that are manifest and come at us directly—can also be a rich source of going-in stories. When I was in high school, one of my classmates was given the unfortunate sobriquet of "Schnozz." The constant taunting by his fellow students created an ugly duckling going-in story on his part, and this, in turn, led him to become a shy, inwardly focused adult. His fellow students' taunts became his story; his story became his life.

The explicit environment of a business organization can be just as damaging. I once did some consulting for a professional services firm that prided itself on hiring "brainiacs." These highly verbal, highly competitive people loved nothing more than trying to outdo one another at trading barbs. As the CEO told me, "In this company, sarcasm is the language of affection." But not everyone was as "affectionate" as the CEO and his coterie. Those individuals who weren't as quick-witted were often the butt of jokes and soon began to feel insecure. Quite a few of them developed the story that they were intellectually inferior. They weren't able to deconstruct the story until they moved on to companies where true intelligence and performance, not mean-spirited competition, were valued.

As we go through life, additional negative experiences give birth to new going-in stories. When these stories persist even as our circumstances change, *they become core limiting beliefs*. They act as self-censors that constrict our behavior, filling us with doubts that keep us from breaking out of old, destructive patterns:

- "I've had a bad temper ever since I was a kid; I'll never be able to control it."
- "I can't ask her out; I'm too boring to interest her."
- "I didn't get very good grades in high school; I'd probably flunk out of college if I went back."

- "I'm just not comfortable enough to express myself publicly; for me, silence is golden."
- "I could never manage people; I'm better off not applying for that promotion."

As I mentioned earlier, I am not a psychologist. I avoid delving into the intimate details of my clients' personal lives and early childhood experiences. Instead, I try to get them to depersonalize their stories. I ask them, "Why do you think you chose to create that story? What's your hunch about that?" Remember the executive who was terrified that conflict on his team would result in his losing complete control? I didn't ask him whether or not this fear could have come from his family situation. I asked him general questions, and he came to that conclusion on his own, which is as it should be. As a coach, my charge is to help individuals uncover their stories and recognize that they may be based not on reality, but on nonrational beliefs.

As a self-coachee, you may find it useful to look back at how you came to believe what you do about yourself and the world around you. Doing so may make it easier to rid yourself of your stories and your core limiting beliefs. If so, flip to Action Step 2.3 at the end of the chapter and try to answer the questions listed there.

Reevaluate Your Stories

As a business coach, I spend a lot of time debunking my clients' stories. It's easy for me, as an outsider, to see the fallacy of some of the beliefs that people hold on to. And, when I repeat their stories as they appear to me, they usually see the fallacy as well. In this, exaggeration is a useful tool. For example, if I were coaching the individual who got fired because he spoke too candidly, I might say to him, "So, you are telling me that everybody, in every company, wants to hear lies, and anyone who tells the truth is fired." Put that way, it would sound patently absurd to me—and to the executive. He would realize that he had taken one event and *overgeneralized* from it, without a scintilla of evidence to support the story.

Along with overgeneralization, *catastrophizing* is another source of nonrational stories. The individual who created a universal law from his one experience of telling the truth was guilty of this as well. Even if it were true that managers don't like to hear the truth, would every manager *fire* an individual who "spoke the truth to power"? That's hardly likely. I would have pointed out this flaw in the person's thinking, thereby putting another story to rest.

To return to the female executive who believed that her colleagues treated her differently because of her race, she too was guilty of overgeneralization. I pointed out to her that there were several other African Americans in the division and that they too viewed her as aloof and unapproachable. It took a while, but eventually she realized that she had no empirical evidence to support her claims of racism.

As your self-coach, you are going to have to be the one to debunk your stories, and for this it's best to elicit the support of your Guide. It will require stepping back, as I do, and looking at each story in a totally depersonalized way. Do this by flipping to Action Step 2.4 at the end of the chapter.

Weigh the Payoffs and Costs

Why do we hold on to our stories, even when we suspect that they are invalid and know that they are imposing limits on us? The answer is simple: every story comes with payoffs. If your story is that you don't have the right last name to get a promotion or that you aren't smart enough to get into the college of your choice or enough of a "salesperson" to make a speech, you never have to risk rejection. You can remain safely in your cocoon and never have to put your ego on the line.

Stories about addictive or self-destructive behavior also have payoffs. If your story is that stopping smoking will make you fat, you can tell the world that you have a valid reason for continuing to get that nicotine high. If you tell yourself that you can't lose weight because you have a thyroid problem, you can keep consuming the calories without much guilt. No matter what your addiction, if you create a story that rationalizes your dependency, you will never have to suffer the discomfort of withdrawal.

Maybe you've been meaning to go back to college and complete your degree or to retake the bar exam that you failed the first time around. You've been meaning to, but it's so hard to study at the end of a long day at the office. And it's not really fair to your spouse for you to spend every night at the library. Better to wait a couple of years, until the kids are older. Rationalization? Yep! No pain, no sweat. Putting your brain into idle and your life on autopilot does have its rewards.

Notice a pattern? I did, early in my coaching career, and I continue to see it. Stories are designed to lock us into our comfort zone. They keep us from making tough choices and the changes they represent. They are our layer of protection from the mental, emotional, or physical discomfort that we so often experience when we are faced with change. Talk about payoff!

But stories have costs as well as payoffs. Often, going-in stories provide short-term benefits, which make them especially seductive. Payment doesn't come until much later. When you're 18 years old, a double cheeseburger and jumbo fries have immediate belly appeal. Who's thinking about the consequences 20 years out? "Take the cash and let the credit go," counseled poet Omar Khayyam, and many of us are all too willing to take his advice.

As a business coach, I spend a lot of time helping clients identify the payoffs and costs of their stories. Here, again, my job is to get the coachee to look at the story in a depersonalized manner. I ask, "What would be the payoff for someone to hold on to a story like that? And what would be the price he would pay?"

The person who was afraid of telling the truth would soon realize that by keeping his own counsel he was avoiding controversy—a definite plus. But, on the negative side, he was ensuring that he was never going to be viewed as a forthright leader who had the courage of his convictions. By playing it safe, he was, in fact, marginalizing himself and making it highly unlikely that he would ever rise to a position of leadership in his new company.

The female executive who tried to play the race card eventually realized that the payoff of her story was that she could go on believing that she wasn't responsible for the way people viewed her. Since it wasn't her fault, why change her behavior? The cost: as long as she continued to devalue people, she would never have their support or cooperation.

Like a profit and loss (P&L) statement, the bottom line of which tells you whether you are in the red or the black, a comparison of the payoffs and costs of your stories reveals their relative merits and why it is important for you to put your stories behind you once and for all. Flip to Action Step 2.5 at the end of this chapter to run a P&L statement on each of your stories.

Create New Stories

Change is about making choices. Once you are conscious of your going-in stories, you are finally in a position to change them. Do the costs outweigh the payoffs? Is the cost/payoff gap so wide that you feel a sense of urgency to reframe your thinking? If so, you've arrived at the "ouch moment." Or, in the language of Ellis's REBT, you are ready to replace your Irrational Beliefs with Rational Beliefs. Your replacement, or "New You," stories are going to be everything that your former ones weren't: based on evidence, not emotion; objective, not subjective; uplifting, not defeatist. For example:

- If you've been telling yourself that you can't go back to school because of other priorities, your New You story will be, "Going back to school is my number-one priority. I will explain to my spouse and children how, in the long run, it will benefit all of us. Now that I am totally committed, I will find the time and energy to complete my degree. I will assess my situation, put some things on hold, and devote less time and energy to others until I complete my degree."
- If you've been using a medical problem as an excuse for not losing weight, you'll seek medical attention. If your doctor says

it's okay, your New You story will be, "I am a normal, healthy person who can lose as much weight as I want to."

- And the weight-conscious smoker would say, "Yes, I will probably gain some weight when I stop smoking. But I will counteract it by eating more carefully and getting regular exercise."
- The replacement story of the individual who thought that telling the truth would get him in trouble might be, "Management in this company wants the truth; by being honest and candid, I will demonstrate my integrity and will be valued more for it."
- Once the black female executive replaced her negative story with one that said, "They are as comfortable with me as they are with anyone else," she was able to focus on the real issues and attain a higher level of impact.

Flip to Action Step 2.6 at the end of this chapter to rewrite your stories.

Now that you've got a plan for dealing with the going-in stories that have been holding you back, it's time to take action. But, before you do, take a minute to review the list of Top 10 Intention-Busting Stories. Add your own favorites to the list!

The Top 10 Intention-Busting Stories

1. It's not possible.
2. I don't have the ability to do that.
3. I'm not good enough.
4. I've failed in the past; why fight destiny?
5. It's too hard.
6. It will take too much time.
7. I have too many other things to do right now.
8. It's not realistic.
9. I'm not ready yet—maybe next year.
10. It's too risky.

JUMP INTO ACTION

Human beings, like all objects, are subject to the force of inertia. Once we are at rest, we will stay put until something jolts us into movement. And once we begin moving, we have a tendency to keep going. It's time to break out of your inertia.

You have clearly set your Intention; you are committed to and passionate about realizing it; you have completed P&L statements on your stories; and you have created new stories that are aligned with your Intention. The question is, "*What is the first step I should take* now *to realize my Intention?*"

Keep it realistic. One small step for a man—or a woman—can be a great leap forward. As the Chinese say, "A journey of ten thousand miles starts with the first step." For example:

- If you want to build your leadership skills, begin by searching the Internet or dropping into your local bookstore to check out the most popular books in the management development area.
- If you've been meaning to go back to college, first visit your local campus and pick up next semester's class schedule. Or arrange to talk to the admissions office to find out what the process is for submitting an application.
- If you've been putting off taking the bar exam again, your first step might be to find out when the next prep classes are taking place and sign up.
- If you're determined to finally stop smoking, start by making an appointment with your doctor to find out what smoking-cessation aids she can prescribe. Log on to the Web site of the American Cancer Society or the American Lung Association to find support groups in your area.
- If you want to improve your relationship with your kids, initiate the process by making sure that all next week's meetings end by 5 p.m. and that you leave the office in time to get home for dinner with the family.

Decide what the first step you will take toward your Intention will be, and flip to Action Step 2.7 at the end of the chapter to write it down.

DECLARE YOUR INTENTION AGAIN

You've come a long way since you announced your Intention. Since then, you've given a good deal of thought and added a good deal of content to your original goal. You've envisioned the end state down to the last detail, and you've begun to live as though you have already achieved your happy ending.

You have also done a lot of soul-searching to uncover and debunk the self-imposed stories and core limiting beliefs that are likely to hinder you as you move toward the fulfillment of your Intention. You have made concrete plans to replace those limiting stories with ones that will enhance your ability to make your Intention a reality.

And you have taken at least one action to put an end to your inertia.

At this point, I recommend that you go back to the people you informed previously and bring them up to date on your progress. This will serve two purposes: first, it will serve as proof of the seriousness of your Intention, and second, it will provide them with more information on the self-coaching process that you will be following—a process in which some of them will be intimately involved.

In the next chapter, we are going to ask you to identify a "Circle of Support," which will probably include the people you have already informed, as well as others who will join you on your upcoming journey.

Before we talk about "Choosing Your Travel Companions," there are a few more points that need to be made about Intention.

HOW TO SPOT A COUNTERFEIT INTENTION

The results you get are proof of your Intention. In my experience, that statement is right on target. When the executives I coach fail to make the changes in behavior for which we have contracted, it's nearly always because their Intention isn't a true one; it is counterfeit. In other words, their actions are not congruent with the Intention that they have expressed.

As I pointed out earlier, counterfeit Intentions are most common when the coaching has been set up or recommended by a third party. Sometimes, executives who have been sent to a coach by management to "get fixed" will go through the motions, but their heart isn't in it. Deep down, they don't see a need to change, and they don't change. After nearly three decades of executive coaching, I've gotten pretty good at spotting counterfeit Intentions early on. And, when I do, I let management know that this person isn't coachable. It's time to pull the plug.

But even when clients know that it's in their best interest to change and *think* that they want to, their Intention may not be as firm as they profess. I'm currently coaching the president of a firm who is dealing with a dysfunctional partner. When we began working together, my coachee professed an Intention to take control of the situation and no longer allow this person to ride roughshod over him and the rest of the management team. To date, however, he has been unable to bring himself to confront the offender. During our last coaching session, I pointed out that he was not manifesting the Intention he had set with me. "If your Intention was to manifest 'powerful leader,'" I told him, "you aren't succeeding. You have an objective, on paper, but that's as far as it goes." His response was a classic example of catastrophizing: "If I confront him directly, he may leave, and the business really needs him." That's the story that he's hiding behind to keep from doing what he knows he should.

You would think that when we sign up, of our own volition, for a self-improvement program—and often make a hefty financial investment in it—we would feel more of a commitment to see it through. But counterfeit Intentions prevail in the life-coaching arena as well. In our mind, we know that we need to make a change. We understand, on the rational level, why our current behavior or life situation isn't ideal and how it could be improved, but we still resist. As Werner Erhard puts it, we "run a racket": we say that we want to change, but we never take action. If I am saying that my Intention is to quit cigarettes, but I continue to slip away for a smoke periodically, my real Intention is to continue puffing. If I say that my Intention is to be a better listener, but I cut off my spouse every time she expresses an opinion, then I don't show up as a good listener—proving that my real Intention is not to be one.

As we continue to exhibit this incongruent behavior, we rationalize our failure to achieve our Intention by falling back on our stories and creating new ones to make the failure acceptable.

Think back to Oprah Winfrey's public remorse about regaining the weight she had struggled to get off. She explained her relapse by saying that she had gone through some serious health problems and, "I felt completely defeated. . . . I was so frustrated that I started eating whatever I wanted. My drug of choice is food. I use food for the same reasons an addict uses drugs: to comfort, to soothe, to ease stress."[9]

What I take away from Oprah's explanation is that her Intention to lose weight was, at bottom, counterfeit. Way down deep, she was holding on to the story that she could stay thin as long as she didn't feel defeated or frustrated. Once that happened, she needed to get solace from food. As long as she held on to that story, she was never going to be able to keep her weight down permanently.

In the same article, Oprah went on to say that she had had a new "aha!":

> When I stop and ask myself, "What am I really hungry for?" the answer is always "I'm hungry for balance, I'm hungry to do something other than work." If you look at your overscheduled routine and realize, like I did, that you're just going and going and that your work and obligations have become a substitute for life, then you have no one else to blame. Only you can take the reins back. That's what I'm doing. These days I've put myself back on my own priority list; I try to do at least one hour of exercise five or six days a week. As I work out, eat healthfully, and reorder

my life so there's time to replenish my energy, I continue to do the spiritual and emotional work to conquer this battle once and for all.[10]

Oprah has replaced the story that food is a cure for emotional distress with one that says, "Food is not the solution to my problems; when I am upset or frustrated, I will find another way to feel better."

Leaving aside my concern that Oprah will merely "try" to exercise five or six days a week, her new story is a positive one. Her challenge going forward will be to develop and commit to a clear Intention, as I have defined it, and to keep her old story from regaining control. We wish her well this time around.

KEEPING YOUR INTENTION STRONG

Keep Your Intention Strong By . . .

- **Building it into your vocabulary**
- **Encouraging those around you to ask about your progress toward your Intention**
- **Keeping it alive on Twitter and Facebook**
- **At the end of each day, entering into a journal every action—no matter how small—that you took that day to move your Intention forward**
- **Doing something "out of the box," for example, imagining a Post-it glued to your forehead, displaying your Intention for the whole world to see**

Oprah is not alone in her struggle to resist turning to food in times of stress and distress. When the going gets tough, people have a tendency to retreat to their comfort zone and, like Oprah, find solace in familiar behaviors.

All of us have an inner and an outer voice. Our outer voice is the one that professes our Intention to the world. It's the voice of reason and determination. Our inner voice, on the other hand, is often a negative one, filled with irrationality and hesitation. This negative inner voice may speak to us when our rational self is most vulnerable: when we are tired, frustrated, angry, disappointed, or depressed. Messages from our negative inner voice can undermine our Intention.

I like the advice that Wayne Dyer gives regarding our inner voice:

> *Monitor your inner dialogue.* Notice how much of your inner speech focuses on what's missing, the negative circumstances, the past, the opinions of others. The more cognizant you become of your inner speech, the sooner you'll be able to shift right in the midst of those habitual inner proceedings. . . . That new inner dialogue becomes the link connecting you to intention."[11]

I know from personal experience that this advice works. I've gotten up on many a morning and hesitated before doing my 50 push-ups. My negative inner voice says, "I went to bed late and I'm too tired" or "I've got to get to the office early today; I don't have time" or "It won't matter if I miss one day." I recall one morning when I had to write a proposal before 9 a.m. I got to the office early and was in the middle of writing it when I realized that I hadn't done my push-ups. My negative inner voice said, "Don't stop now; you've got to get this proposal done." But, because I was conscious of how my nonrational self was trying to sabotage my own Intention, and because I am so committed to that Intention, I was able to ignore its siren song. I took off my shoes and dress shirt, dropped to the floor, and did my push-ups.

Another tip for dealing with your negative inner voice: ban words and thoughts like "try," "maybe," "hopefully," "with luck," or "we'll see." The vocabulary of uncertainty is nothing more than an attempt by your irrational self to dilute the power of your Intention. For example, trying is *not* the same as doing. Participants in our leadership programs realize the truth of this statement when we ask them to "try to pick up a pencil." Each time they reach for the pencil, we stop them, saying, "Don't pick it up; *try* to pick it up." The experience barrels home the distinction.

Each time a doubt about your ability to achieve your Intention surfaces, refuse to accept it. Replace it with a positive thought: "I will pass that exam"; "I will be able to control my overeating"; "I will get that promotion."

Joe Wions discovered the power of positive thinking several years into his battle with ALS:

> I have pretty consistently held to the notion throughout this ordeal that recovery (at some level) is a possibility. The flaw in this way of thinking is that, if reversing this disease is a "possibility," then the opposite is also a "possibility." ALS is a neurological disorder, and the brain is the center of the nervous system. If my brain is sending out messages to the rest of the system that recovery is only an "option," then my potential for recovery has been compromised. So, my strategy going forward is to convince myself that recovery is a certainty, and that it has already begun.[12]

But is an especially seditious word in your inner dialogue. I choose not to say, "I've got to do 50 push-ups, *but* I'm in a rush this morning." That formulation implies that I've already found an excuse for releasing me from the obligation to myself. Rewording the statement to, "I've got to do 50 push-ups, *and* I'm in a rush," gives it a whole new connotation. In this formulation, being in a rush no longer precludes my doing my push-ups. This is a subtle, but important distinction to someone who is trying to outsmart his negative inner voice.

Do you talk to yourself? Try it! A "dialogue between self and soul," in the words of poet Archibald MacLeish, can be your Intention-saver. Talk to your inner voice. Take it on. Confront it. Speak out loud to it with your voice of reason and determination: "Why are you whispering to me? I won't back down."

Deadly Inner Voices

The Inner Critic. You want to go to college? With the grades you got in high school?

The Cynic. You've never been able to stop drinking. What makes you think you'll do it this time?

The Procrastinator. I'll just finish this one pack before I quit.

The Fatalist. I'm not even going to apply for that job. There's no way they'd ever hire me.

The Racketeer. I hate my job, but I can't look for a new one while I'm working, and I can't afford to quit this one. I'm between a rock and a hard place.

The Rationalizer. I didn't want dessert, but it would have been rude to refuse.

The Pollyanna. Don't worry, be happy. What's a Ph.D. going to do for you, anyway?

The Night Watchman. Change isn't welcome around here. Keep out!

I'd like to end this chapter as it began, with a quote from my friend Joe Wions. Joe has kept his Intention—and himself—alive, against all odds. He has been tempted many times to abandon that Intention, but he has never given in:

> Every day I have to remind myself of the choice I'm making and to behave in a manner that is consistent with that choice. I have chosen to find a way to defeat what doctors call an always-terminal illness. Every time my breathing becomes more labored or my arm becomes more difficult to move, it tests my resolve to live up to the choice I have made and to believe in the possibility of my success. It is daunting, at times, to maintain that positive mind-set in the face of evidence to the contrary and limited evidence of progress in the direction of my choice.[13]

There is no way to prove that Joe's Intention is what has kept him alive 10 years after the onset of ALS, but there is no doubt that it has enhanced the quality of his life. The strength of his Intention has attracted an entire network of caring individuals who have formed a Circle of Support around Joe.

In the next chapter, "Choosing Your Traveling Companions," we'll discuss Step 3: how you too can create a Circle of Support to help you keep your Intention alive.

Action Step 2.1: What Is Your Intention?

The clearest way to state your Intention is to make sure that it contains three elements: an action, an end result, and a time frame. For example, lose 30 pounds in six months; complete my bachelor's degree in two semesters; fly a plane solo in one year.

If your Intention is to eliminate some negative behavior, don't focus on what you are giving up; instead, think about what you will be gaining. Include a fourth element: the positive outcome that you expect. For example, lose 30 pounds in six months in order to fit into last year's wardrobe; quit smoking in three months so that I'll live long enough to see my son graduate from college.

Write your Intention on a sheet of paper, or enter it on www.coachyourselftowin.com, stating it as a complete thought: action, end result, time frame and, if applicable, positive outcome.

Action Step 2.2: To Whom Will You Declare Your Intention?

On a sheet of paper or on www.coachyourselftowin.com, list as many people as you can think of to whom you will declare the Intention that you just set. When making your list, include all those who can provide one or more of the following: moral support, an attentive ear, subject-matter expertise, feedback, personal experience in achieving this Intention, or introductions or connections.

Some of these people may be casual acquaintances with whom you'll have little or no further contact; others will no doubt become part of the Circle of Support that you will be creating later on. At this point, don't worry about forging a long-term relationship with them; just tell them about your Intention. However, try to avoid announcing your Intention to "naysayers"—those who are unlikely to support, and may even sabotage, your efforts.

Action Step 2.3: What Are Your Stories and Where Do They Come From?

Think about the Intention you set earlier in this chapter. Write your answers to the following questions on a sheet of paper, or enter them on www.coachyourselftowin.com.

1. What doubts are you feeling about your ability to achieve this Intention?
2. What going-in stories do these doubts suggest? What beliefs are you holding on to that may keep you from achieving your Intention?
3. How did I come to create this story? What was the original event or experience in my life that brought it about? Enter your answers into the table provided on www.coachyourselftowin.com. If you are writing your answers on paper, make a table with two columns, one for "Story" and one for "Triggering Event," to organize your answer.

Action Step 2.4: Evaluate Your Stories

Refer to the list that you made in Action Step 2.3. Read each story and evaluate it as objectively as possible. Be brutally honest with yourself, as I am with clients. Do you have evidence to support it? Are you overgeneralizing based on one past experience? Are you catastrophizing—painting the worst possible picture of what will happen if you try to achieve your Intention? Are the insurmountable obstacles really "out there" or are they internal barriers that you have set up?

Use the table on www.coachyourselftowin.com or, if you are writing your responses on paper, make a table with four columns, "Your Story," "Supporting Evidence," "Disconfirming Evidence," and "Conclusion," to organize your answers.

Action Step 2.5: Write Up Your Stories' "P&L Statements"

Look once again at your list of stories from the previous exercises, and run a P&L on each of them. Identify the payoffs and costs of each. Are most of the payoffs short-term ones? Have you been ignoring the costs because you aren't likely to have to pay them anytime soon? What's the bottom line for each story?

Enter your responses into the table on www.coachyourselftowin.com, or make a written table with four columns, "Story," "Payoffs," "Costs," and "Conclusions," to organize your answers.

Action Step 2.6: Write Your "New You" Stories

Once again, without a coach to help you frame your New You stories, you will have to rely primarily on your own imagination and ingenuity. You can be guided, however, by one overarching question. For each New You story that replaces an invalid one, ask yourself: "What story will be most helpful to me as I try to realize my Intention?" Enter your responses into the table on www.coachyourselftowin.com. If writing your responses, make a table with two columns, "Old Story" and "New You Story," to organize your answers.

Action Step 2.7: What's Your First Step?

Write down, or enter on www.coachyourselftowin.com, one step that you will take immediately to start moving toward your Intention.

CHAPTER 3

CHOOSING YOUR TRAVELING COMPANIONS

The Self-Coaching Process
Determine Your Self-Coachability
1
Select and Commit to an Intention
2
Identify Your Guide and Circle of Support
3
Solicit Feedback
4
Analyze and Respond to Feedback
5
Develop and Act on a Game Plan
6
Track Your Success and Recalibrate
7

Back in the early 1960s, 22-year-old Herm Rowland and his parents were the owners of the Herman Goelitz Candy Company, an Oakland, California, candy-manufacturing business founded by Herm's grandfather. Despite its reputation for quality and its modest annual growth rate, the company yielded only a minimal profit. Today, the Herman Goelitz Candy Company is known as the Jelly Belly Candy Company, maker of the world-famous, flavor-rich gourmet jelly beans that have delighted everyone from toddlers to adults, including President Ronald Reagan, for more than 30 years. Each year, Jelly Belly produces more than 34 million pounds of tasty treats, including more than 50 varieties of jelly beans in flavors ranging from bubble gum to kiwi. With nearly 800,000 square feet of production facilities in its two U.S. factories, Jelly Belly also makes candy corn, chocolates, gummies, sour candies, and other tasty confections.[1]

How did the Rowlands achieve this phenomenal success?

It began with lunchtime meetings at the family factory with a man named Mr. McDaniel. Herm recalls McDaniel as being "all business," yet genuinely concerned about helping the family turn the business around. And there were no shortage of issues to tackle.

The family was operating its business out of a cramped 10,000-square-foot building where it was impossible to work efficiently. Herm recalls that McDaniel encouraged him and his parents to expand, even though profits were negligible. McDaniel guided them through the process of securing a loan, moving to a larger factory, and revamping their merchandising and costing system. McDaniel provided Herm with practical business tools and wisdom that would prove invaluable as Herm guided the company through the next decade and prepared to introduce gourmet jelly beans in 1976.

Although he lost contact with McDaniel many years ago, Herm, who is now chairman and CEO of Jelly Belly, likes to think that

McDaniel would be smiling if he could see how far the company has progressed.[2]

Just who was this mysterious Mr. McDaniel who served as a mentor, or Guide, for Herm and his family?

McDaniel was, in fact, a retired operations and finance executive who had worked for a Utah salt manufacturer. At the time he helped the Rowlands, he was a volunteer with SCORE, the Service Corps of Retired Executives. Launched by the Small Business Administration (SBA) in 1964 as a nationwide resource group, SCORE began with 2,000 volunteers and now has more than 11,000. These retirees offer their assistance free of charge to small business owners who, like the Rowlands, are in need of guidance. SCORE is just one of several SBA programs for small, minority, and female-owned businesses. Through them, individuals whose Intention is to start a new business or make an existing one more successful can find Guides like Mr. McDaniel to help them make their dream a reality.

Back in Chapter 1, we compared embarking on a self-coaching program to taking a leap of faith: venturing into new, uncharted territory. History is full of stories of explorers and pioneers who hiked, sailed, rode, or flew into the unknown. The wisest and most successful of them didn't make the journey on their own; they took traveling companions who were willing to share their knowledge and experience. Lewis and Clark were guided by Sacajawea in their exploration of the Louisiana Purchase; Sir Edmund Hillary engaged Sherpa Tenzing Norgay to accompany him on his ascent of Mt. Everest; every safari into the heart of Africa was led by a native guide. In literature, too, there's a long tradition of following a Guide on a momentous journey. In the *Divine Comedy*, Dante actually had *two* Guides: the Roman poet Virgil took him through Hell and Purgatory, and his ideal woman, Beatrice, showed him the way to Heaven.

Likewise, there's no reason for you to embark on your self-coaching journey alone. After all, what is unknown to you may be quite familiar to others. Why not benefit from their experience? "Only the fool learns from his own mistakes; the wise man learns from the mistakes of others." It's an old saying and very true. Trying to go it alone is one of the biggest reasons that people fail to achieve their Intentions.

I never coach an executive in a vacuum; every coaching assignment includes a *mentor* and a number of *stakeholders*. There are several reasons for this:

- First, without questioning others, it is impossible to get a true picture of the behavior that needs to be changed. It's also impossible to determine whether or not coaching is actually resulting in behavior change unless you have witnesses who can attest to it. Those around us provide what sociologist C. H. Cooley called a "looking-glass self."[3] You size yourself up through the perception of others.

- Second, collective brainpower trumps that of a single individual. As Michel de Montaigne observed more than 500 years ago, "It is good to rub and polish our brains against that of others."[4] The mentor and stakeholders are a rich source of suggestions and strategies for success that might never occur to the coachee or even to the consultant.

- Third, it's a big morale booster to know that you aren't alone on your journey. If your enthusiasm starts to flag, your mentor and stakeholders will be there to cheer you on. If you start to lose your way, they'll point you back in the right direction. When you reach your goal, they'll be there for the celebration.

In the discussion of self-coaching, I will be using the term *Guide* instead of mentor and *Circle of Support* instead of stakeholders to designate the individuals who will be joining you on your journey. Before I describe your relationship with them, let me explain how the mentor and the stakeholders contribute to the business-coaching process. The discussion should enrich your understanding of the business counterparts of your Guide and Circle of Support. Let's begin with the mentor.

THE MENTOR IN BUSINESS COACHING

The word *mentor* comes from the name of a character in Homer's *Odyssey.* The original Mentor was the wise old friend of Odysseus who remained behind when the Greeks sailed off to fight in the Trojan War. Odysseus had so much faith in Mentor's ability and judgment that he entrusted his entire household, and also the upbringing of his son, to this giver of sage advice.

Since the time of Homer, the term *mentor* has come to refer to someone who can provide valuable information and advice, or counsel, to less-experienced individuals. For centuries, master craftsmen served as mentors, passing on their trade to apprentices and journeymen. In the heyday of sailing ships, boys signed on for round-the-world voyages with a captain who taught them how to navigate. In religious orders, acolytes and novices received instruction from and followed the example of the ordained clergy. Today, the mentor system is alive and well, as student teachers, medical interns and residents, and apprentices learn the ropes from those who have gone before them.

In the business world, a mentor can help a new hire navigate the unknown waters of the organization. He can shed light on internal politics, unspoken rules, and "the way things get done around here." Having a good mentor can make the difference between a steep learning curve and a meteoric rise through the ranks.

For an executive who is receiving coaching from an outside consultant, a mentor is an equally important source of support. The mentor offers advice, lends moral support, observes and provides feedback on the coachee's progress, and smooths the way when the going gets rough. The mentor is, in effect, a source of forward thrust as the coachee moves toward her Intention.

CHOOSING A MENTOR

To carry out these duties successfully, a mentor must be someone

- Whom the coachee trusts and respects
- With whom the coachee is comfortable

- Who is in a position to observe the coachee's on-the-job behavior consistently
- Who doesn't hold back and will not hesitate to give the coachee candid feedback
- Who has the coachee's best interests and success at heart

Approximately 40 percent of the time, our coaching services are requested by the executive himself. In these instances, the individual is seeking to acquire additional skills that will propel him to the next step: become more adept at influencing others, be seen as a more powerful leader, improve his conflict management skills, or learn to think strategically. We are called in to impart these skills.

The remainder of the time, the request for coaching comes from the executive's boss or one of the company's HR professionals, in response to a perceived issue or opportunity. In the most difficult cases, these individuals have noticed or been told about behavior on the part of the executive that is interfering with her ability to perform on the job. Such behavior runs the gamut from being too aggressive to being nonassertive, from failing to follow through on commitments to not insisting that others do so, from merely failing to recognize others' contributions to actually taking credit for their accomplishments. You name it, we've coached people through it.

Once we have contracted to carry out the coaching, a mentor needs to be chosen. In a business setting, the number of people who are in a position to observe the coachee's on-the-job behavior day in and day out is usually limited, making the choice of a mentor fairly straightforward. The role usually goes to one of the two individuals who may have called us in: either the person to whom the coachee reports or the HR "gatekeeper" who works most closely with the coachee's business unit. On rare occasions, such as when there are major issues between the coachee and his boss and an HR professional is not available or appropriate, another executive may be called upon to serve as mentor.

When I first meet with the coachee, her mentor is present. The three of us discuss the general observations or aspirations that have led to the coaching intervention. Together, we project what success will look like. If we have contracted to replace existing behaviors, we ask, "What new behaviors will replace the old, dysfunctional ones?" If the executive wants to take her game to a new level, we focus on the question, "What new skills do you want to possess at the end of the coaching experience?" We then select those colleagues of the coachee—the stakeholders, about whom we'll say more in a little while—from whom we will solicit more data on the coachee's current behaviors and/or suggestions for ways to improve the coachee's performance.

It is my responsibility, as the coach of record, to draw up the questions that I will ask the stakeholders, and also to summarize the information that they give me and feed it back to the coachee. The mentor is present when I give the feedback to the coachee, so that he has a complete picture of what needs to be accomplished. The three of us then develop a plan to either begin replacing the behaviors in question or develop the needed skills. Finally, we agree on a schedule of phone calls and visits during which we will track progress on the plan.

One of the most important roles of the mentor is that of "shadow coach." Since I am present only at scheduled intervals, my opportunity to observe the coachee and provide real-time feedback is limited. In my absence, the mentor acts as another set of eyes and ears, noting and pointing out both progress and setbacks. In some cases, he can provide suggestions for dealing with the latter in real time; at other times, all the mentor can do is make sure that the issue is addressed in our next three-way phone call or face-to-face meeting.

In my career as an executive coach, I've met several mentors who stand out in my memory because they added so much value to the coaching process:

- I was brought in to coach one executive who was not perceived as having a sense of urgency. It required constant prodding to get him to take action, and his first reaction was to make excuses for his failure to do so. His boss was an excellent mentor. Whenever she saw that he was slacking off and making excuses, she didn't hesitate to say, "It seems like you are still playing out the same game." Her feedback was timely and specific, and included distinctions: "Your project plan is already a week overdue, and you're telling me that it's because you haven't gotten the vacation schedule from HR. If you were keeping your commitment to change your behavior, you would have gone to HR two weeks ago and made sure they had the schedule completed before your deadline."

- In another case, my coachee often alienated his coworkers by his aggressive interpersonal style. The first time I sat down with him and his mentor, he immediately began to defend and justify his behavior. His mentor was having none of it. She countered with, "The way you are reacting to this feedback is the same way you behave with others. You show up as unreceptive to them. You believe that you need to justify your behavior, so you come across as being more interested in explaining yourself than in getting their point of view. Why is that?" She continued to hold his feet to the fire, asking one provocative question after another until he stopped talking and started listening.
- A third executive had a difficult time influencing those over whom she had no direct control. She always felt that she had to go to her boss for assistance when she had cross-functional issues. In my initial meeting with her and her boss, who was serving as her mentor, the boss went right to the heart of the issue, saying, "I want to be here for you when you really need me, but you *always* seem to delegate your issues with people outside the department to me. Why do you do that? How else could you resolve these issues?" His questions forced the coachee to think about her behavior, the story behind it, and alternative ways of thinking and acting.

I know a mentor is doing a great job when I deliver feedback and the coachee responds with, "I know. I've already talked about that with my mentor," or when I check in and the coachee opens the conversation with, "My mentor suggested that you and I discuss . . ."

THE GUIDE IN SELF-COACHING

When I asked you to determine whether or not you could coach yourself to win, one of the "musts" that I said you needed was a mentor, or Guide: *someone who is in a position to observe your progress and help you stay on track.* I assume that there is someone in your life who is willing and able to play this role.

Because, as a self-coachee, you will not have a consultant to lead you on your journey, your Guide will have to take a larger and more active role than the mentor in the business-coaching model. So will you. Figure 3.1 shows how the roles and responsibilities included in the self-coaching process will be divided and/or shared between you and your Guide.

CHOOSING YOUR GUIDE

Looking at the many ways in which your Guide will assist you, it's evident that he must be a very special person, one who is willing to invest the time and energy to help you reach your Intention. A Guide should have the same qualities as a business mentor—and then some. The ideal Guide would be

- Someone whom you admire and respect
- Someone with whom you are comfortable sharing your deepest hopes and dreams—and fears
- Easy to talk to, a good listener who doesn't interrupt while you are making a point
- A positive person, not a naysayer or a pessimist
- Someone whose only vested interest is in your success

The Self-Coaching Process: Roles and Responsibilities	Self-Coachee	Guide
Test the realism of the Intention.	×	×
Select a Circle of Support and craft the message to them.	×	×
Formulate questions to elicit data from the Circle of Support.	×	×
Collect data from the Circle of Support.	×	
Analyze responses.	×	×
Develop a plan.	×	×
Share the plan with the Circle of Support	×	
Provide the self-coachee with real-time feedback.		×
Monitor the self-coachee's progress against the plan.	×	×
Solicit feedback on progress from the Circle of Support.	×	If asked to by coachee
At predetermined intervals, ask the Circle of Support to assess the self-coachee's progress.	×	
If needed, develop a plan of corrective action.	×	×

FIGURE 3.1 The Self-Coaching Process: Roles and Responsibilities

- Someone who is not afraid to "go there"—who will give you the unvarnished truth about your behavior, your "stories," and your lapses
- Someone who suggests instead of prescribing
- A good questioner, whose questions are designed to get you to think of your own solutions

- Thoughtful; someone who doesn't rush to judgment or action without considering the facts carefully
- Unafraid of change, viewing it not as a threat, but as an opportunity for growth
- Intellectually curious
- Someone who has enough time and a flexible enough schedule to be there when you need her
- Someone with a good sense of humor, who can relieve the tension with a laugh
- A subject-matter expert; someone who has special knowledge/experience in the area in which you are self-coaching

At this point, you may be saying, "But I don't know anyone who has all those qualities." Maybe not, but I'm sure you know several people who each have *some* of them. Look at the list again: Which characteristics are most important to you? Do you think it's more important to have a Guide who has subject-matter expertise ("been there, done that") or someone who, although he has no firsthand experience of your Intention, is intellectually curious enough to want to learn all about it with you? Do you yourself tend to be pessimistic? If so, having an optimist as a Guide might be far more important than having a good questioner. Your own nature and the nature of your Intention must be considered as you seek a Guide who *approximates* the ideal.

Reviewing this list, I know exactly whom I would choose as my Guide if I were in hot pursuit of an Intention: my friend David. David and I have been friends since grammar school. I admire how he has led his life and pursued his goals. He is highly ethical, he keeps his promises, and we share the same values. We have an excellent rapport and, through the years, we have often talked about our hopes and dreams for the future, along with our concerns and fears about our ability to achieve them. He is committed to his own personal growth, and I know he is committed to mine.

Knowing how demanding my schedule is, he would be willing to work with me at odd hours, whenever I needed him. He loves me like a brother, but he doesn't hesitate to hold up a mirror to me to point out my failings. He takes risks, but they are always *considered* risks. He's a doer, but he's also a thinker. And he knows how to make me laugh.

It may also be helpful to select as a Guide someone who has had the same Intention as you and has reached it. You might be able to avoid some of the wrong turns and dead ends that she took on the journey. But be careful: no two people are exactly alike, and the path your Guide took may not be the right one for you.

Who shouldn't be your Guide? Obviously, anyone who has the opposite characteristics from those we just described. For example, another friend of mine, Tom, has been married for 10 years and has two children, ages eight and six. He and his wife have been having problems since the birth of the youngest, and about a year ago he finally decided to move out and start divorce proceedings. After a month on his own, he gave in to his wife's pleas that he return home. Since then, he's moved out two more times, but each time his wife has lured him back with the promise that she'll go to couples therapy, change the behavior that drives him crazy, and so on.

Tom has a large extended family and lots of friends. He shouldn't have had any problem finding a Guide, but most of the people around him were hard taskmasters. His mother and sisters voiced the opinion that he was a "patsy" and a "jerk" for moving back. His father shook his head in disappointment and dismay at his son's "spinelessness." His best friend was outraged when he learned that Tom's wife had broken three appointments in a row with their counselor. His advice: get out of Dodge today, file for divorce tomorrow, and don't look back. After a couple of months of this ego-pounding and tough talk, Tom shut down. He declared the subject of his marriage off limits and refused to "go there" with any of them.

Clearly, Tom is not ready to deliver the "shock and awe" treatment to his wife. He obviously didn't do the soul-searching he should have done before setting his Intention. At this point, Tom doesn't need people putting him down, berating him for his failure, or pushing their alternatives on him. He needs someone who will help him ask the important questions and answer them honestly. He needs to become aware of the payoffs and costs of staying and how they compare to those of leaving.

I was happy to hear recently that Tom seems to have finally found the cool-headed, nonjudgmental Guide that he needs. The husband of one of his sisters stepped up and offered his support. (Someone who's not a blood relative usually finds it much easier to depersonalize.) Tom was elated as he related to me the many ways in which Elliot has already helped him.

"He's the only one who didn't say, 'I can't believe you haven't gotten this nailed down yet. You're nuts,'" Tom recounted. "He listens to me and asks questions that make me think about what I really want and why I can't seem to go for it."

Evidently, Elliot is especially good at questioning—one of the key skills for a Guide. The other people in Tom's circle are always asking him, "Why did you do that?" "Don't you realize what a mistake that was?" "How could you let that happen?" and similar "questions" that are disguised put-downs and value judgments. Elliot's questions, according to Tom, focus not on the mistakes that Tom has made but on the steps that he is going to take to get back on track: "What are you going to do next?" "Are you going to stay on this path, or have you changed your mind?" "If so, why?" With Elliott's guidance, Tom now stands a good chance of resolving his marital problems once and for all.

Here are a few more caveats about choosing your Guide. Avoid selecting a co-conspirator as your Guide. If you're trying to stay sober, don't enlist a drinking buddy; if you are trying to lose weight, don't stick with a Guide who suggests you talk about your progress at the local pizzeria. You don't want a Guide who's a rescuer, who insists on speaking and acting on your behalf. Nor do you want someone who "triangulates" by going to your other supporters and discussing your foibles and failures with them.

A Guide

Is . . .	Is not . . .
an advisor	an enabler
a questioner	an answer-giver
a listener	a doer
a sounding board	an echo
an advocate	an excuse maker
a mirror of your behavior	a judge of it
a monitor of progress	a taskmaster
"you" focused	focused on him- or herself

When it comes to choosing a Guide and a Circle of Support, you, as a self-coachee, have a lot more options than the executives to whom we provide coaching services. Here are just a few of the sources you should consider when selecting your Guide:

- Longtime friends
- Family members, both immediate (be careful here; remember Tom's experience) and extended
- Close neighbors
- Fellow hobbyists
- People you know through community organizations, alumni groups, or professional societies

- If your Intention relates to your career: your boss, executives in other departments or divisions, clients or vendors with whom you have a close relationship, or a former colleague who has been promoted or moved to another organization
- Your religious/spiritual advisor

Think about these and any other sources of Guides that are open to you. Then think about the qualities that you want—and don't want—in your Guide. Flip to Action Step 3.1 at the end of the chapter to analyze your choice.

WORKING WITH YOUR GUIDE

When you're choosing a Guide, it's important to set some firm ground rules before you begin to work together. Selfimprovement base.com is an Internet portal that describes many resources that are available to people who are embarking on a self-help program: books, articles, DVDs, audio programs, and so on. The site contains some excellent advice on how to make the mentor-mentee relationship work.

Here are some of the tips that can be found there. I've replaced the word *mentor* with *Guide*, since that's the term we'll be using.

- Openness, honesty, realistic expectations, accountability, and ability to admit mistakes and failures make for a good relationship.
- Set boundaries relating to confidentiality and time commitments.
- Do not overburden your Guide by demanding too much attention from him or her, or becoming overly dependent.
- The relationship is especially productive when the Guide believes he or she can learn from you, and thus the relationship becomes mutually beneficial.

- Express that you value and appreciate your Guide's guidance. The feeling of being needed and making a difference in a protégé's life will often be a rewarding payoff for the Guide, but don't be afraid to supplement that appreciation with a token gift, flowers, or by picking up the bill when you share a meal. Sometimes a simple note is enough to praise your Guide for his or her contribution to your professional growth.[5]

Remember, we're not talking here about a mentor or Guide whom you pay for services. You are asking someone who cares about you to donate her time and energy, *gratis*. It's important that you approach this person correctly and explain your request clearly.

- If your chosen Guide wasn't among those to whom you already announced your Intention, state what it is and why it is important to you.
- Tell the Guide that you are embarking on a self-coaching program, and that he is one of the people you would most like to join you on this journey of discovery. You will be asking others to come along as well, but you want him to be your main supporter.
- Tell the person what steps you have already taken: announced your Intention to others, begun living in your Intention, uncovered your stories and their payoffs and costs, replaced them with "New You" stories, and taken at least one action to start moving toward your Intention.
- Explain the remaining steps in the self-coaching process.
- Explain the role you are asking the person to play.
- Give the person your best estimate of the time commitment you will need from him.
- Set the ground rules (when and where you will meet, how often, and so on).

Flip to Action Step 3.2 at the end of the chapter and explain how you will discuss your Intention with your Guide.

Now that you've secured your Guide, let's talk about the rest of the people who sign on for the journey: the stakeholders in executive coaching and the Circle of Support in self-coaching.

THE STAKEHOLDERS IN BUSINESS COACHING

Back in Chapter 2, I introduced you to Steve, the human resources executive in a Fortune 100 company who was promoted and whose COO recommended that I coach him through the transition period. As you'll recall, because of Steve's low-key, nonassertive personality, his colleagues had trouble perceiving him as a powerful leader.

Here's the rest of the story. The COO had recommended that Steve be promoted to head up HR in the Asia/Pacific Region. He had great faith in Steve's ability to take on the wider challenge, based on the camaraderie that Steve had built and the stellar results he had achieved in the United States. But shortly after Steve assumed his new position, the COO began hearing rumblings from the region heads. Their major concern: Steve was too U.S.-centric. The COO decided to mentor Steve and, as part of his development program, arranged for me to coach him.

The first thing I did was formally gather feedback from the stakeholders who had commented on Steve's "U.S.-centric" behavior. This group included the members of the International Leadership Team: the heads of the six geographic areas in which the company operated and the corporate support staff. They gave me specific examples of Steve's ethnocentric behavior: using analogies that only an American would understand, peppering his speech with American slang, using U.S. sports examples to illustrate points, and scheduling meetings and phone calls without regard to time-zone differences and non-U.S. holidays. They said that, in general, Steve seemed uncomfortable in his new environment, which caused his colleagues in the region to view him as "all business" and someone who lacked the personal touch. They did an excellent job of zeroing in on all the areas in which Steve needed to change his game.

I gave Steve their feedback and discussed with him and his mentor a plan for going forward. Steve then went back to each of the stakeholders; thanked them for their candid, constructive comments; and invited them to continue giving him feedback as he attempted to change. He asked them to let him know both when they saw him falling back into his old habits and when he was successful at demonstrating cultural sensitivity.

During the next few months, as Steve became more comfortable in his new global role, these stakeholders remained actively engaged in his development. They offered alternative examples and phrases that would be more universally accepted than those that Steve habitually used. After each meeting in which they saw him in action, they pointed out slips and successes. They served as a sort of kitchen cabinet while Steve made the transformation from all-American to citizen of the world.

The interaction I have just described is typical of the way in which stakeholders contribute to the business-coaching process when it is led by an outside consultant. As the example demonstrates, stakeholders play two major roles in executive coaching:

1. **They give you a baseline on the coachee's current behavior**. The consultant solicits input from each of the stakeholders individually, in order to get a clear picture of the behaviors that the coachee needs to change or the skills that she needs to develop. As in the case of Steve, I always ask stakeholders to back up their comments. I keep the focus on their sensory apparatus: What did they see and hear? I attempt to convert "empty-calorie" statements, such as "She has a bad attitude" or "He is not trustworthy," into concrete examples: What evidence do you have? Can you give me an example? (For example, "She keeps customers waiting while she talks to friends on the telephone" or "I have told him things in confidence and later learned that he has repeated them to

coworkers.") The more specific the examples, the more effective the actions that I can plan later on with the coachee and mentor.

2. **They evaluate progress as the coaching proceeds**. As the coachee implements the plan, I check in periodically with the stakeholders, asking them for evidence that the coaching is producing the desired results. I ask them, "Has the coachee made the planned changes? If not, what needs to be done?"

The members of Steve's group didn't limit their feedback to answering my questions at regular intervals. They took Steve's invitation seriously: they provided him with real-time, ongoing feedback at the "teachable moment." They went even further than most groups by giving Steve concrete suggestions for projecting a more global image. And they demonstrated their interest in seeing him win by applauding his progress.

CHOOSING STAKEHOLDERS

The ideal stakeholder possesses the same qualities as the best mentors. As you may recall, he must be someone

- Whom the coachee trusts and respects
- With whom the coachee is comfortable
- Who is in a position to consistently observe the coachee's on-the-job behavior
- Who doesn't hold back and will not hesitate to give the coachee candid feedback
- Who has the coachee's best interests and success at heart

But in the world of executive coaching, the choice of stakeholders is limited. There are only a certain number of people with whom an executive interacts often enough and closely enough for them to be able to judge her progress. Working with the coachee and the mentor, I usually identify from eight to twelve colleagues who meet the criteria and who can give me a 360-degree view of the coachee.

Given these limitations, executives who happen to work in a tight-knit, friendly business unit, as Steve did, are fortunate. In less friendly, more formal environments, stakeholders may not provide as much support. But it is up to the coach/consultant to ensure that they honor their commitment to deliver ongoing, honest feedback in a nonthreatening way.

Once the stakeholders have been identified, I help the coachee craft an e-mail informing them that he is going to be coached by Guttman Development Strategies, Inc., and that the GDS coach is going to be scheduling meetings, of approximately 45 minutes each, with each of them to get their input before the coaching begins. The letter tells each stakeholder that as one of those who interacts frequently with the coachee, she can provide valuable information on the coachee's situation and needs. It explains that the coachee will receive only a summary of the feedback and that none of the comments will be attributed to a specific individual, so the stakeholder need not be concerned about confidentiality. The coachee also indicates that he will personally get back to each stakeholder after discussing the summary and resulting plan with the coach.

Fortunately, as a self-coachee, you will have a much wider and deeper pool from which to draw your Circle of Supporters, as well as several options for the way in which you enroll its members.

THE CIRCLE OF SUPPORT IN SELF-COACHING

It's impossible to overstate the importance of having a Circle of Support during the self-coaching process. Two of the most successful behavior-changing programs of our time, Weight Watchers and Alcoholics Anonymous (as well as numerous others that have adopted their model), were founded on this premise. People who are addicted to food have a tendency to withdraw from others. "Food addicts love to isolate themselves, where no one can see what they consider to be their unattractive bodies. When alone, food addicts can binge in peace, smothering any unpleasant feelings with a grocery-cart-full of food."[6] Many alcoholics are also solitary drinkers, preferring the company of the bottle to that of their friends and family.

Attending weekly meetings with people who share the same Intention forces these self-coachees, which is what they really are, out of their self-imposed isolation. It's painful at the outset, but in the end it empowers them: they celebrate with fellow members who have had a good week, buoy up and remotivate those who haven't done so well, and share personal tips that have helped them through the previous seven days. If there is a group leader, that person is another valuable resource, contributing the knowledge that she has gained from working with past groups, or perhaps being a member of one.

Addicts aren't the only ones who benefit from declaring their Intention to others and asking for their help. Many people say that they want to change things, but never do. One reason for their failure is that they don't declare themselves publicly: they don't invite people to support them. Instead, they hide out and try to go it alone in order to avoid the performance pressure that comes from social interaction. When you enlist a Circle of Support, you put yourself "out there." Circle members know if you aren't following your plan, and they will call you on it. Putting yourself on the line demonstrates a significant commitment to your Intention and represents a major step forward along the pathway to realizing your happy ending.

Executives who don't put themselves on the line with their stakeholders never get the benefit of the group's collective brainpower. Many self-coachees also fail to benefit from a support group because people often feel shy about asking for help. We fear rejection or showing up as weak and needy. But recall St. Matthew's advice: "Ask, and it shall be given you; seek, and ye shall find; knock, and it shall be opened unto you."[7]

Knock with confidence when you ask someone to join your Circle of Support. Think of it as extending an invitation to accompany you on an important journey. Only a trusted few are invited to travel with you. Let the prospective Circle members know that the journey will not cost them much in money or in time. There are gifts that are far more precious than these that you want them to bring along: you want their wisdom, insight, and capacity for emotional support as you move along the pathway to fulfilling your Intention.

Knock at their door. Tell them about your Intention and why you so fervently seek its fulfillment. Let them know that they are special and that you value them. Then ask them to join you. You'll be surprised at how willing they will be and how much "shall be given you."

Knocking to invite people into your Circle is no sign of weakness. It takes great ego strength to admit that you don't have all the answers. It also tells those around you that you're serious about making a change and that you are smart enough to realize that self-coaching doesn't mean *solo* coaching. Your Circle of Support provides the power boost that you may need if and when the going gets rough.

EXTENDING THE INVITATION

I am 59 years old and, as I mentioned earlier, I am in pretty good shape. I complete at least 50 push-ups every morning, and I also lift weights, bike, hike, kayak, and swim. From time to time, I've toyed with the idea of entering a triathlon. I haven't yet set a serious Intention to do so, but if I ever do, here's how I will go about enrolling my Guide and my Circle of Support.

I will, of course, ask my oldest and best friend, David, to be my Guide, for the reasons I enumerated earlier. I will then sit down with David and brainstorm about the people who would be most likely to help me realize my Intention. They will probably include my wife; my brother, who is my professional trainer; and a friend who is a nutritionist. I will probably also try to identify someone who has successfully competed in triathlons and ask that person to join my Circle.

Because I'm a very outgoing person and I like "happenings," I will invite these people to dinner at my home. Sometime after we've eaten, when everyone's sitting around relaxing, I will make my announcement. Maybe I'll start with that old chestnut, "I suppose you're all wondering why I've asked you here." Maybe not. But I will tell them that I am going to be embarking on an exciting journey: I am going to be coaching myself to achieve a goal that means a great deal to me. I would like all of them to be my traveling companions on this journey:

"My Intention is to compete in a triathlon. I've thought long and hard about it, and I am very serious and highly committed to this Intention. It's important to me because it will confirm the success of another Intention that I have had all my adult life: to maintain my good health and strength in order to continue to engage in the physical activity I enjoy so much."

I will continue by saying, "I trust all of you; I know I can count on you to be there for me. I believe that your input will be of great value to me as I work toward this goal."

Next, I will explain what I am asking of them. To begin, I'd like them to answer some questions about what they see as my strengths and weaknesses, both mental and physical; the barriers I'm likely to run into; the actions that they suggest I take to overcome these barriers; and any other information that they can supply that will empower me as I go forward. I'll let them know that, afterwards, I'd like to check in with them once a month to discuss my progress and get their best thinking on what I need to do next. I will continue to do this until I have reached my goal.

Finally, I'll explain the unique role that David is going to play as my Guide: primary sounding board, advisor, and "go-to guy." I will tell them that David and I will develop a list of questions for them to answer. I'll outline the ground rules:

- Setting a date and time when we can meet in person
- Sending each person the questions in advance
- Along with the questions, sending a brief set of guidelines to help them answer the questions

I'll invite questions from my guests about my Intention and the self-coaching process that I'm going to be following. I'll test their buy-in by asking them if they will commit to joining me on the quest.

If any of my chosen supporters aren't willing or able to participate, I'll thank them for listening and then look for a replacement.

Not everyone has the same sense of high drama that I do or is as comfortable as I am in a social setting. Nor is it always possible or practical to get your entire Circle of Support together for a formal kickoff to your self-coaching. There are no hard-and-fast rules for how to inform your Circle of Support. If you would prefer to meet with each person individually, that's fine. Just make sure that in each interaction, you

1. State your Intention and why it is important to you.
2. Acknowledge the person as a valued partner; give her permission to be totally open and honest with you.
3. Clearly explain the role that you are asking the person to play *at the beginning and throughout the self-coaching process*: give you an honest picture of where you are now compared to where you want to be vis-à-vis your Intention; provide periodic, ongoing feedback on your progress: things you're doing right and areas where you need to improve; and share with you any suggestions that she may have to facilitate your achievement of your Intention.
4. Ask the person if she is willing to be a part of your Circle of Support.

5. Establish ground rules for how often you will communicate with the person. Let her know that you will continue to call on each person in your Circle, individually, at regular intervals, until you have realized your Intention. Tell the person that if you fail to check in as promised, she shouldn't feel any hesitation about initiating the contact.
6. Tell the person the name of your Guide and explain his role: like the rest of your Circle, the Guide is going to be a source of initial and ongoing feedback, but he will also be your primary sounding board and advisor.
7. Let the person know who else has agreed to join your Circle.
8. Mention the fact that you are going to be providing her with a packet of materials to use when delivering her feedback.
9. Answer any questions that the person has about the process going forward.

If I ever decide to go for my dream of competing in a triathlon, at the end of my dinner party, I will tell my Circle of Support that we won't all be together again for a while. The next time I invite them all to dinner, it will be to celebrate my achievement and their contribution.

However you choose to tell your Circle that you've reached your Intention and their job is over, make sure that you let them know how deeply grateful you are for the help that they gave you during your journey.

CHOOSING YOUR CIRCLE OF SUPPORT

Many of the criteria you should use to select your Circle of Support are the same ones used to select stakeholders in business coaching. Primarily, *both groups must be made up of people who are willing to "put themselves at stake" for your success.* In other words, they care about the outcome that you achieve and will do everything in their power to help you win.

Let's take another look at the criteria I gave earlier for choosing a Guide:

- Someone whom you admire and respect
- Someone with whom you are comfortable sharing your deepest hopes and dreams—and fears
- Easy to talk to, a good listener who doesn't interrupt while you are making a point
- A positive person, not a naysayer or a pessimist
- Someone who really wants you to succeed
- Someone who is not afraid to "go there"—who will give you the unvarnished truth about your behavior, your "stories," and your lapses
- Someone who suggests instead of prescribing
- A good questioner, whose questions are designed to get you to think of your own solutions
- Thoughtful; someone who doesn't rush to judgment or action without considering the facts carefully
- Unafraid of change, viewing it not as a threat, but as an opportunity for growth
- Intellectually curious
- Someone who has enough time and a flexible enough schedule to be there when you need him
- Someone with a good sense of humor, who can relieve the tension with a laugh
- A subject-matter expert; someone who has special knowledge/experience in the area in which you are self-coaching

The same criteria apply to the choice of your Circle of Support, although in most cases you will be asking for a lot less of their time and advice. The same caveats also apply: no co-conspirators, rescuers, triangulators, and so on. And, as in the case of your Guide, it is highly unlikely that every member of your Circle will possess every one of these traits. Try to find people who possess those that are most important for you and your Intention. Whatever you do, don't fail to invite someone into your Circle because she isn't the perfect choice.

I don't mean to pick on Oprah Winfrey, whom I admire greatly, but I wonder whom she has chosen to support her. I believe that Bob Greene is her personal weight-loss trainer and that through the years he has devised various diet and exercise plans for her. I know that there are a number of people who appear on her program who are her good friends, including her longtime best friend, Gayle King; cardiothoracic surgeon Dr. Mehmet Oz; and spiritual activist Marianne Williamson. In spite of what would seem to be an excellent support network, she continues to have trouble achieving the permanent behavior change that she is pursuing. She herself has admitted that the story she has been holding on to has gotten in the way of her success. I can't help but wonder if her friends and advisors function effectively for her. For example, have they ever

- Challenged her stories?
- Held her accountable for behaving in accordance with what she says that she wants?
- Pointed it out to her every time they've seen her go astray?
- Felt as though she wouldn't break when they gave her feedback, so they didn't have to pull any punches?
- Asked her the tough questions that she hasn't been willing or able to ask herself?
- Checked in with her, even if she didn't call them, to see whether or not her plan was working?
- Cheered her on, step by step, when she has made progress?

If those around her haven't been supporting her in these ways, I'd suggest that she explore with them the reasons why and what they can do together to change their approach.

How many people should you ask to join your Circle? My answer is, "the fewest needed." If your goal is a simple one, such as stopping smoking or losing weight (I said "simple," not "easy"), you might need only two or three people: your doctor, a member of your immediate family, and perhaps a good friend.

If your Intention is a complex one, like changing careers, you may need a larger Circle—say five or six. You may also decide, sometime after you've chosen your Circle, that you need to add members because you have entered a new stage in your self-coaching. For example, you may reach a point in your preparation for a new career where you need to acquire new skills, which may entail attending a workshop or engaging a private tutor. Subject-matter experts of all kinds, paid and unpaid, can add significant value as Circle members. Or you may join a group like Weight Watchers or AA for added support. In my own case, I work with a trainer who knows how to add challenging elements to my workouts, in carefully thought-out phases, so that I don't risk injury. He was a valuable resource as I worked up to my Intention of doing 50 push-ups every day.

You can canvass the same sources as you did for your Guide, plus a few others:

- Longtime friends
- Family members, both immediate and extended
- Close neighbors
- Fellow hobbyists
- People you know through community organizations, alumni groups, or professional societies
- Your religious or spiritual advisor
- If your Intention relates to your career: your boss and close colleagues as well as those in other departments or divisions, clients or vendors with whom you have a close relationship, or a former colleague who has been promoted or moved to another organization

- Local organizations, such as vocational schools, business schools, and colleges
- Support groups, such as Weight Watchers, Overeaters Anonymous, AA, and Al-Anon
- Adult education classes

Don't limit yourself to people in your immediate physical vicinity. Before I moved to Cleveland to get my M.S. at Case Western Reserve University, I set an Intention to get a job in the museum world when I returned to New Jersey. I selected a Circle of Support: four thought leaders in the field who were all well connected and who cared about me. I asked one of them to serve as my Guide. I contracted with all four before I left for graduate school, promising to correspond with them once a quarter. I did that religiously throughout the time I was away from the East Coast. As a result, I had several options when I graduated, and I got the job I wanted because one member of my Circle provided the connection.

That was back in 1975, and the correspondence that I conducted with my Circle was by phone and surface mail. How times have changed! In today's virtual world, there is almost no limit to the resources you can access. E-mail has made it cheap and easy to correspond with good friends who live in other parts of the country or abroad. Like-minded individuals can enroll in Yahoo! or Google Groups on any subject. You can blog and tweet about your Intention, post it on Facebook, and talk about it in a video on YouTube. While some of these forums are far too public and superficial for a serious self-coachee, others are excellent places to find tips and moral support from others with the same Intention.

One of these forums is the *New York Times*'s blog spot, where I came across the story of an overweight, unfit couch potato in Brooklyn who got fed up with his own poor physical condition:

> Tomasz Berezinski awoke after a night of inebriety with a headache and decided his life must change. He started running, bought a GPS device and turned his body into a brush and the

> city into his canvas. . . . Since that morning almost a year ago, Mr. Berezinski, 40, has run three marathons, lost 16 pounds and taken to creating huge drawings by following routes through city streets in the shape of faces, dogs and anything else that strikes his fancy. After planning a route, he traces it on foot or bicycle carrying his GPS device to record his progress. Then he uploads the "drawing" he has made to a map-sharing site called everytrail .com. Part sport, part art, GPS drawing lets runners, walkers, cyclists and hikers imagine themselves anew—not just as a collection of burning muscles, sweaty armpits, forward motion; not just as people endeavoring to crest a hill or lose five pounds. Instead, they are neo-cartographers, jumbo-size doodlers and bipedal pencils, mapping their track lines across cities, roads and farms, and sharing them online.[8]

What a great way to reenergize yourself when you grow weary of following the path to your Intention: map out a new route and take off on it!

Choosing Your Circle of Support: The Seven Deadly Sins

- Choosing people who won't be straight with you
- Choosing people who don't care about you
- Choosing those who are duplicitous, who highjack the process and make it their issue
- Choosing people who don't have time for you
- Giving in to your own tendency to pick people who will go easy on you and tell you what you want to hear
- Settling because you are afraid that the best people are too busy or not interested in you
- Not choosing because you can't find the "perfect" fit

Take some time to think about the roles, characteristics, and examples of Circle members that we have been discussing here, then flip to Action Step 3.3 at the end of the chapter and answer the questions there about your Circle of Support. Ask your Guide to help you think through your answers.

ANOTHER WORD ABOUT YOUR GUIDE AND CIRCLE OF SUPPORT

The biggest mistake that a Guide and Circle of Support can make is to not hold the self-coachee accountable for his own success. All too often, misguided supporters take the monkey off the back of the self-coachee and onto their own shoulders. Don't let the monkey migrate!

As an executive coach, I know that I cannot change the person I am coaching. No one can change another person. The role of the consultant, mentor, and stakeholders in business coaching and that of the Guide and Circle of Support in self-coaching are much more subtle: empowering the person who is undergoing the coaching to change herself.

George Cook, another SCORE volunteer, helped Patricia Miller, cofounder of Vera Bradley Designs, to grow her company exponentially. He did it, says Patricia, not by prescribing but by empowering:

> George never told us what to do or how to do it. He would ask questions that helped us find the solutions ourselves.[9]

In the next chapter, "What's the Message?" we'll talk about how you begin to tap into the resources of your Guide and Circle of Support to find the solutions that are right for you.

Action Step 3.1: Who Will Be Your Guide?

On a separate sheet of paper or on www.coachyourselftowin.com, answer the following questions.

1. Whom will you choose to be your Guide as you self-coach toward the Intention you set in Chapter 2?
2. What characteristics does this person possess that make him or her a good choice?
3. Are there any potential problems with choosing this person as your Guide? If so, what are they, and can you find a way around them?
4. If your initial choice for your Guide is unable to accept the role, whom will you choose as a backup?

Action Step 3.2: Discussing Your Intention with Your Guide

Write down or enter on www.coachyourselftowin.com what you plan to say to your chosen guide about your Intention and his or her role in helping you achieve it.

Action Step 3.3: Who Will Be in Your Circle of Support?

Write down or enter on www.coachyourselftowin.com the names of the people whom you will ask to join your Circle of Support.

Note: It's best to assume that not everyone will accept your invitation. I suggest that you have an A list and a B list in case your first choices fall through.

1. What characteristics does each of these people possess? What value can each add?

   Enter your responses into the table on www.coachyourselftowin.com or, if you are writing your answers, make a table with two columns, "Individual" and "Characteristics/Value," to help you organize them.

2. Are there any potential problems with any of your selections?

For example, the person is too judgmental, isn't likely to have enough time, is too close to you to be objective, or has some other problem.

If answering in writing, make a table with two columns, "Individual" and "Potential Problem(s), to help you organize your answers.

3. Are any of these potential problems serious enough for you to disqualify the person? If so, can you come up with a replacement?

If writing your responses, make a table with two columns, "Problematic Individual" and "Replacement," to help you organize your answers.

Now that you have selected your Circle of Support, discuss with your Guide the pros and cons of speaking to the members as a group versus speaking to each member individually. Enter your responses on www.coachyourselftowin.com or on a sheet of paper.

4. How do you plan to enroll your Circle of Support? Will you bring them all together, or will you approach each one individually?

With your Guide, craft and record on our Web site or on paper the message that you will deliver to the members of your Circle.

5. What will you say to them about the self-coaching process, your Intention, and their role in helping you achieve it?

CHAPTER
4

WHAT'S THE MESSAGE?

The Self-Coaching Process
1 Determine Your Self-Coachability
2 Select and Commit to an Intention
3 Identify Your Guide and Circle of Support
4 Solicit Feedback
5 Analyze and Respond to Feedback
6 Develop and Act on a Game Plan
7 Track Your Success and Recalibrate

The book on Steve:

Steve . . .

You are very much respected for your intelligence, commitment, creativity, calm demeanor, communication/people skills, and analytical ability. Overall, you are seen as a talented individual who has a lot to offer the company. Nevertheless, in the interviews, there were several themes that surfaced around developmental opportunities. These include

Demonstrating Effective Leadership. You are perceived as needing to be more assertive and to demonstrate a clearer, more commanding leadership presence. You need to be seen not only as a transactional manager, but as a driver of initiatives. Many commented that you should connect often with your predecessor, who was quite successful in this position, for feedback and advice.

Building Collaborative Business Partnerships. You need to spend time connecting with the stakeholders and your business partners within the region, as well as with corporate headquarters. Many of those surveyed indicated that one of your key challenges will be to effectively navigate and manage a variety of cultures within the region. Although you did this successfully within the Africa/Middle East Region, the complexity of both the cultural and business issues within the Asia/Pacific Region will require you to spend time learning the business, while also building a functional HR team. Responses reflected both confidence and concerns regarding your ability to do this.

The expectation is that you will operate as a decisive leader who will build a strong HR team, help drive initiatives, and develop effective collaborative business partnerships with the stakeholders and the corporate office.

Respondents to this survey are very positive about you and what you bring to the organization. They value your HR expertise and experience and have high expectations regarding this role within the region. Your ability to contribute further to the success of the organization requires that you utilize the coaching experience as a method to expand and build upon your strengths, while addressing some important areas for further development.

These paragraphs were taken from a Feedback Summary that was recently compiled for the executive we've been referring to as Steve, the HR executive in a Fortune 100 company who was promoted and whose boss recommended that I coach him through the transition period. Because he was so low-key and nonassertive, Steve's colleagues had trouble perceiving him as powerful. As you'll recall, one of the exercises I asked him to complete was to envision, down to the last detail, what it would look like if he were to show up as a powerful leader.

The data in Steve's Feedback Summary came from 11 people: his mentor and 10 stakeholders, including the heads of the company's Human Resources Department and its Asia/Pacific Region. I conducted personal interviews with each, then sat down with Steve to analyze the responses and extrapolate major themes, which are incorporated in the Feedback Summary.

As I stated earlier, there are three "musts" for successful self-coaching:

- Accurate data, so that you understand the current "actual" and what winning looks like
- A Guide in the loop, someone who is in a position to observe your progress and help you stay on track
- The willingness to go beyond your comfort zone, to drop your defenses and become open to feedback, to take a leap of faith in order to improve your life

We begin every business-coaching assignment by gathering the most accurate data we can find and, as a self-coachee, you must do the same. "If you don't know where you are going, any road will take you there." This is as true for a coaching journey as it is for travel plans. Without clear, accurate pictures of where the coachee currently stands and of her ultimate destination, it's impossible to chart the correct course—that is, to choose the right actions to bring about the desired behavior.

Feedback paints those pictures for the business coach, and it does the same for the self-coachee. In this chapter, we are going to examine the process by which accurate data are gathered, analyzed, and responded to.

WHAT IS FEEDBACK?

Feedback is a verbal or nonverbal communication to a person that provides the recipient with information regarding *how his behavior is affecting others*.

In our executive coaching, we are interested only in behavior that affects the coachee's own ability, along with the ability of others in her workplace, to achieve the desired *business results*. Behavior that interferes with the ability to get the job done is counterproductive, and the goal of coaching is to replace it with more effective behavior.

If your Intention relates to improving your on-the-job performance, you too will be focused on gathering information about your *workplace behavior* and *how it affects business results*.

If your Intention is not business-related, but relates to how well you are performing in other areas of your life, you will still be seeking information about your *behavior*, but it will be about *how that behavior affects you, your family and friends, and everyone else with whom you come into contact on a regular basis*. You'll be trying to unearth data about how the things you do, consciously or unconsciously, affect your ability to achieve the results you desire: a happy marriage, a good relationship with your children, close friendships, a better-paying job, optimum health and longevity, recognition for your talents, more time to enjoy life, and so on.

How can you ensure that you get the most useful feedback and that you respond to it in a way that will move you closer to your Intention?

SOLICITING FEEDBACK

As a self-coachee, you will be following the same steps that we go through when we gather and respond to feedback from an executive coachee's mentor and stakeholders, with minor variations.

The left column of Figure 4.1 lists the steps that we go through in business coaching; the corresponding steps in self-coaching are listed on the right.

Business Coaching	Self-Coaching
1. **Framing the Questions** Generic questions are customized by coach.	1. **Framing the Questions*** Generic questions are customized by self-coachee and Guide.
2. **Collecting the Data** Coach meets individually with each stakeholder and with mentor to gather feedback.	2. **Collecting the Data** **Option 1 (preferred):** Self-coachee meets individually with each member of Circle of Support and with Guide to gather feedback. **Option 2:** To preserve anonymity, Guide and Circle of Support complete questionnaires and submit anonymously online.
3. **Analyzing the Data** Coach analyzes data, compiles written Feedback Summary.	3. **Analyzing the Data** **Option 1 (preferred):** Self-coachee and Guide analyze data and compile informal written summary. **Option 2:** GDS consolidates online responses of Circle and sends back to self-coachee.
4. **Constructing the Plan** Coach and coachee construct the coachee's Personal Development Plan (PDP).	4. **Constructing the Plan** Self-coachee and Guide construct the coachee's Personal Development Plan (PDP).
5. **Closing the Loop** Coachee shares highlights of PDP with each stakeholder.	5. **Closing the Loop** Self-coachee shares highlights of PDP with each member of Circle.
* To create either a questionnaire that you can print out and distribute to your Circle or one that Circle members can complete anonymously online, go to our Web site, www.coachyourselftowin.com.	

FIGURE 4.1 Process for Soliciting Feedback and Responding to It

In this chapter, we will look at the first two steps in the process, those that deal with soliciting feedback, and will highlight the similarities and differences between what we do as business coaches and what you will be doing as a self-coachee. In Chapter 5, we will do the same for Steps 3 to 5, which deal with responding to feedback.

FRAMING THE QUESTIONS

In business coaching, once the stakeholders have been enrolled, the coach looks at the generic set of questions that Guttman Development Strategies, Inc. (GDS) typically uses in coaching and customizes them for the coachee's mentor and stakeholders. Remember, the purpose of gathering these data is to get clear, accurate pictures of the coachee's current behavior and of what a successful outcome would look like. A Personal Development Plan can then be made to close whatever gaps exist between the two.

To get these pictures, we must ask each stakeholder the same questions. We may vary the questions a bit, depending on whether the stakeholder is a peer, a direct report, or a supervisor. We may also add a few individualized questions if we know that the coachee has a particular issue with a stakeholder or if certain stakeholders work more closely with her.

Also, depending on their working relationship with the coachee, some of the stakeholders may not be able to answer all the questions. For example, if one of the issues is how the coachee interacts with his direct reports, an executive from another department, who sees the coachee only in cross-functional meetings, is not likely to have observed such interactions. This is likely to occur in self-coaching as well, as not all members of your Circle will have observed you in all your interactions. You'll need to instruct your Circle, as we do stakeholders, that this is not a problem, and that they can simply proceed to the next question.

How many and what kind of questions do we ask? I probably ask fewer questions than most of the coaches in our firm. I generally find that a dozen or so questions are enough to give me an accurate baseline for understanding what's occurring and what needs to change.

Following is the Feedback Questionnaire we developed for Steve. The answers that his stakeholders gave formed the basis of the Feedback Report that was reproduced at the beginning of this chapter:

1. How would you describe the way Steve has been operating in his new role?
2. How should Steve be operating now that he has been promoted?
3. What key initiatives, actions, or projects does Steve need to focus on to add value in his new role?
4. What one or two actions could Steve take that would make an immediate, positive difference in his performance?
5. What strengths does Steve bring to his role?
6. In what areas does Steve need to improve or develop?
7. What two or three things are most likely to prevent him from succeeding in his new role?
8. What can you, personally, do to help him succeed?
9. Do you know of anyone else in the company who has been successful in this role, and, if so, what can Steve learn from this person?
10. Can you recommend any other sources of support for Steve?
11. On a scale from 1 (Strongly Disagree) to 5 (Strongly Agree), how strongly would you agree with the statement, "Steve is a coachable individual who is likely to reach his Intention"?
12. On a scale from 1 (Strongly Disagree) to 5 (Strongly Agree), how strongly would you agree with the statement, "I feel comfortable providing Steve with honest and accurate feedback regarding his Intention"?

There are questions that we consider inappropriate. These include leading questions, such as, "Alice needs to show up as more powerful. What do you know about that?" or "Do you think Joe needs to go to sensitivity training?" The goal of the coach is to come in as a blank slate, with no agenda of her own. The conversation needs to go in the direction in which the stakeholder takes it.

There is also no place, in executive coaching, for questions that go beyond workplace behavior and business relationships. For example, a coach would never ask, "Do you know if Frank is having marital problems?" or "Do you think Deborah drinks too much?" The focus needs to stay on behavior that has been *observed* in the *workplace*. It would be appropriate, however, for the coach to ask, "What counterproductive behavior has Frank demonstrated? What do you think might be causing this behavior?"

For me, the following 12 questions, which are the "generic" form of those we just asked about Steve, yield all the information I need:

1. How would you describe the coachee's current situation or behavior with regard to his/her Intention?
2. What situation or behavior will you see if the coachee is successful?
3. What actions can the coachee take to close the gap between 1 and 2?
4. What one or two actions would make the greatest positive difference in the coachee's efforts to achieve his/her Intention?
5. What strengths does the coachee possess that could help him/her achieve his/her Intention?
6. In what areas does the coachee need to improve or develop?
7. What two to three things should be the greatest "watch outs"—things that are most likely to cause the coachee to derail?

8. What can you, personally, do to help the coachee achieve success?
9. Do you know of anyone else who has achieved the same Intention as the coachee and, if so, what can the coachee learn from this role model?
10. Can you recommend any other sources of support for the coachee?
11. On a scale from 1 (Strongly Disagree) to 5 (Strongly Agree), how strongly would you agree with the statement, "The coachee is a coachable individual"?
12. On a scale from 1 (Strongly Disagree) to 5 (Strongly Agree), how strongly would you agree with the statement, "I feel comfortable providing the coachee with honest and accurate feedback regarding his/her Intention"?

Note: In personal interviews, we suggest that, wherever appropriate, you ask follow-up questions in order to initiate a dialogue that will enable you to gather as much information as possible. For ideas on how to do this, see the "Guidelines for Receiving Feedback" that are provided in Chapter 5.

Let's see how a self-coachee could rephrase these 12 questions to solicit the necessary data in three self-coaching situations, with the following Intentions.

Note: It often helps those being interviewed to depersonalize the situation if you refer to yourself in the third person when asking the questions, as I have done in the following examples.

- **I, Howard Guttman, have set the Intention to be promoted to the next level in the company by this time next year.**

  1. How would you describe the way Howard Guttman carries out his job duties?
  2. If Howard Guttman wanted to get to the next level in this organization, what would his job performance need to look like?

3. What could Howard Guttman do to increase his chances of getting a promotion by this time next year?
4. What one action could Howard Guttman take that would be most likely to help him get a promotion?
5. What are the things that Howard Guttman does best?
6. What skills or work habits does Howard Guttman need to develop in order to get a promotion? What behaviors does he have to stop?
7. What are one or two things that are most likely to keep Howard Guttman from getting a promotion?
8. What can you, as a friend and colleague, do to help Howard Guttman get promoted?
9. Is there anyone else in the company who has received a promotion and whose experience Howard Guttman could learn from?
10. Can you recommend any other sources—people, programs, courses, books, articles, videos, or anything else—that can help Howard Guttman get a promotion?
11. On a scale from 1 (Strongly Disagree) to 5 (Strongly Agree), how strongly would you agree with the statement, "Howard Guttman is a coachable individual"?
12. On a scale from 1 (Strongly Disagree) to 5 (Strongly Agree), how strongly would you agree with the statement, "I feel comfortable providing Howard Guttman with honest and accurate feedback regarding his Intention"?

- **I, John Jones, have set the Intention to stop smoking completely within two months in order to improve my health and extend my life.**

1. How much does John Jones smoke currently?

2. Ceasing smoking completely is the desired outcome. Do you think that John Jones can envision himself as a nonsmoker?

3. What could John Jones do to increase his chances of being able to quit smoking within two months?

4. What one action could John Jones take that would be most likely to help him quit smoking?

5. What traits or behaviors does John Jones demonstrate that might help him quit?

6. Knowing John Jones, what do you think are the major hurdles he'll have to overcome?

7. What are one or two things that are *most* likely to keep John Jones from quitting cigarettes?

8. What can you, as a friend, do to help John Jones stop smoking? What advice would you give him?

9. Is there anyone whom you or John Jones knows who has quit smoking and whose experience John could learn from?

10. Can you recommend any other sources—people, programs, courses, books, articles, videos, or anything else—that can help John Jones stop smoking?

11. On a scale from 1 (Strongly Disagree) to 5 (Strongly Agree), how strongly would you agree with the statement, "John Jones is a coachable individual"?

12. On a scale from 1 (Strongly Disagree) to 5 (Strongly Agree), how strongly would you agree with the statement, "I feel comfortable providing John Jones with honest and accurate feedback regarding his Intention"?

- **I, Sara Smith, have set an Intention to have a better relationship with my spouse within six months.**

  1. Based on what you've seen, how would you describe the way Sara Smith and her spouse interact?
  2. How would Sara Smith and her spouse interact if their relationship were better; in other words, when you look at people whose marriages work well, how do those spouses interact?
  3. What could Sara Smith do to improve her marriage?
  4. What one or two actions could Sara Smith take that would have the greatest positive impact on her marriage?
  5. What traits or behaviors does Sara Smith demonstrate that might help her improve her marital relationship?
  6. Knowing Sara Smith, what do you think are the major hurdles that she'll have to overcome?
  7. What are one or two things that are most likely to keep Sara Smith from making her marriage better?
  8. What can you, personally, do to help Sara Smith improve her marriage? (For example, based on your own marriage, what suggestions do you have for her?)
  9. Is there anyone that you or Sara Smith knows who has turned his or her marriage around and whose experience she could learn from?
  10. Can you recommend any other sources—people, programs, courses, books, articles, videos, or anything else—that can help Sara Smith improve her marriage?
  11. On a scale from 1 (Strongly Disagree) to 5 (Strongly Agree), how strongly would you agree with the statement, "Sara Smith is a coachable individual"?

12. On a scale from 1 (Strongly Disagree) to 5 (Strongly Agree), how strongly would you agree with the statement, "I feel comfortable providing Sara Smith with honest and accurate feedback regarding her Intention"?

Now it's your turn. Flip to Action Step 4.1 at the end of the chapter and personalize the generic questions as we did in the previous examples.

COLLECTING THE DATA

As you can see from the description of each of the steps in Figure 4.1, there are a number of differences between the way data are collected in business coaching and in self-coaching.

In executive coaching, the coach conducts the interviews with the mentor and stakeholders. There are several reasons for this. First, in business situations, where the stakeholders are chosen because of their place on the organization chart rather than their personal relationship with the coachee, it is often easier for them to be candid with a third party. Since they know that the coachee will receive only a Feedback Summary and that no specific comments will be attributed to them, they are more likely to "tell it like it is." Second, professional coaches have excellent questioning skills and the ability to ferret out important information in follow-up questions.

As a self-coachee, you will be assuming this responsibility yourself. *It is not something that you should delegate to your Guide.* After all, one objective of this process is for you to take full responsibility for your own life. This is one step toward that goal.

We also recommend that you plan to speak to each member of your Circle personally. A personal interview enables you to engage in a dialogue; ask follow-up and clarifying questions; and look for hidden messages in body language, facial expressions, and other nonverbal cues. It is also a way to deepen and strengthen your relationships with some of the most important people in your life. By sitting down face to face with them, you are enhancing your ability to communicate on meaningful subjects with those who are closest to you and, eventually, with others. It's a valuable learning experience that you should take advantage of, if at all possible.

However, you may find that one or more members of your Circle are reluctant to speak to you candidly in a face-to-face meeting. For whatever reason, they would prefer to deliver their feedback from a distance, and preferably anonymously. In such cases, which in our experience are the exception rather than the rule, you have several options:

- You can ask the individual(s) who are reluctant to sit down with you face to face if they would be comfortable submitting their written answers and including their name when they return the questionnaire. If they don't insist on anonymity, you can still interview the other members of your Circle personally.
- If one or more individuals insist on anonymity, you will need to instruct *everyone in your Circle* to return the completed questionnaire, without his name, either through the mail or through www.coachyourselftowin.com.

Whichever option you choose, I recommend that you give the members of your Circle of Support some time to think through their answers, and that you also give them some guidelines for delivering feedback.

Businesspeople are generally accustomed to providing feedback on the performance of those who report to them. In addition, they often participate in 360-degree feedback exercises, where they respond to questions about their supervisors and their peers. Many organizations also offer training programs in giving feedback, so employees have some familiarity with the dos and don'ts of the feedback process. Unless your Intention is business-related, it's possible that the members of your Circle will not have had much, if any, experience in this area.

Providing systematic feedback may be a new experience for both your Guide and your Circle of Support. So before they deliver their feedback, give each of them a copy of the Briefing Packet that is included in Action Step 4.2. Not only will it help them to give you more useful information, but it will demonstrate to them that you take their input very seriously.

Knowledge may be power, and self-knowledge may be enlightenment, but unless you convert feedback to action, it is unlikely that you will change your behavior and move toward achieving your Intention. What's the best way to respond to the feedback you have received? We provide answers in the next chapter.

Action Step 4.1: Questions for Your Guide and Circle of Support

Focus once again on the Intention that you set in Chapter 2. On www.coachyourselftowin.com or on a separate sheet of paper, write down your Intention.

Next, sit down with your Guide and discuss the 12 generic questions provided on pages 119–120. How will you rephrase them to get the information you need from your Guide and your Circle of Support? Rewrite the questions on www.coachyourselftowin.com or on paper.

Note: You may find it helpful to draft your personalized Feedback Questionnaire on paper. When you are satisfied with the way the questions are expressed, you can go to www.coachyourselftowin.com and enter them into the template provided there.

Whether or not you plan to have your Guide and Circle complete a hard-copy Feedback Questionnaire, I suggest that you print copies of the completed template and "Guidelines for Delivering Feedback," then distribute them. If you plan to collect the feedback anonymously, you can save your personalized Feedback Questionnaire so that your Guide and Circle can access it at a later date.

Action Item 4.2: Briefing Packet for Your Guide and Circle of Support

Note: Whether you are going to ask your Circle to complete the Feedback Questionnaire online or in hard copy, you are still going to have to log onto www.coachyourselftowin.com to access the templates for your Briefing Packet, which will contain the following three items:

A. *Memorandum: What Is This Feedback All About?*

   You will need to personalize, then print and distribute hard copies of the Memorandum to your Guide and Circle of Support.

B. *Feedback Questionnaire*

   You already personalized your Questionnaire in Action Step 4.1. You can either print hard copies and distribute them with the

Memorandum and Guidelines, or you can direct your Guide and Circle to submit their responses at www.coachyourselftowin.com.

C. *Guidelines for Delivering Feedback*

The Guidelines do not require personalization. They should be printed and distributed along with the Memorandum.

A. Memorandum

Use a separate sheet of paper to organize your thoughts as you personalize the Memorandum, or enter the information directly into the online template.

To:	*Guide and Circle of Support*
From:	*Self-Coachee*
Subject:	*What Is This Feedback All About?*

As I take the next steps toward realizing my Intention of ________________, your support is going to be crucial. Providing me with honest, thoughtful feedback is one of the most important ways that you can help.

Delivering effective feedback can be difficult. I recently came across Coach Yourself to Win, *a book on self-coaching that includes a very useful list of "Guidelines for Delivering Feedback," which I want to share with you. I believe that you will find these guidelines helpful in providing feedback to me and others in your personal and business life.*

[Note to self-coachee: if you have already set a time and place for the in-person interview, you should include that information in this memo.]

I am confirming that I will be meeting with you for a personal feedback session on (day, date, time, place).

[Note to self-coachee: if you haven't yet set the time and place for the in-person meeting, say the following.]

I will be calling you within the next several days to set a time and place for our meeting.

[Note to self-coachee: If people will be providing feedback anonymously on www.coachyourselftowin.com, be sure to give them the Web site address and your password so that they can access your personalized Feedback Questionnaire and read the guidelines. Instructions for registering and receiving a password can be found on the site.]

Once I gather everyone's feedback, I will be back in touch with you to discuss the information I receive from your feedback and that of the other members of my Circle of Support.

I deeply appreciate your willingness to help me achieve my Intention.

Thank you!

B. Feedback Questionnaire

This was completed in Action Step 4.1.

C. Guidelines for Delivering Feedback

Trained observers, who are expert in gathering data and providing feedback, follow a number of rules. They

- Focus on behaviors and identify what they actually see and hear
- Observe overall behavior, not just one incident
- Observe enough behavior to make appropriate judgments
- Create opportunities to observe the person who is being coached

Because you may not have been asked to provide feedback before, we have developed the following guidelines to help you gather and deliver your observations. Please keep them in mind as you deliver your initial feedback and, later on, as you meet periodically with the self-coachee to reassess his or her progress.

1. Give Feedback, Not Feedattack

Feedback is clearly a situation in which the Golden Rule prevails: do unto others as you would have them do unto you. To test whether or not you are adhering to the rule, ask yourself, "Am I giving this feedback in the spirit in which I would want to hear feedback about myself?"

2. Make It "Behavior-Based" and Specific

The most useful feedback is "behavior-based." The goal of coaching is to change behavior, which cannot be done without a clear picture of specific behavior *that has been observed firsthand. Keeping the focus on observed behavior has a number of advantages, including*

- ***Eliminating guesswork.*** *"Unmotivated," "negative," "bad attitude," "short tempered," "childish," "rigid," "lazy," "stupid." People often toss these and other labels around when describing colleagues, family members, and even friends. What they don't realize is that, in themselves, such epithets are meaningless. Even if they are positive—"nice," "smart," "ambitious," and so on—they aren't useful. What constitutes "lazy" or "motivated"? Unless you can describe lazy or motivated behavior, your guess is as good as mine.*
- ***Pinpointing important areas of behavior for improvement.*** *A person can't stop being "lazy" or "negative" or "childish." He or she can only stop lazy or negative or childish behavior. Without knowing what this behavior is, no improvement can ever be made.*
- ***Measuring progress toward an objective.*** *Laziness can't be quantified. Knowing that a person comes in an hour late twice a week gives his supervisor something to work with: getting that figure down to once a week would be an improvement; 30 minutes late would be better than one hour. The ultimate goal: on time five days a week.*
- ***Increasing the chances that the coachee will be receptive to the feedback.*** *Using derogatory labels is tantamount to a personal attack and, when they are attacked, most people immediately*

go on the defensive. They are more interested in defending themselves than in hearing more criticism. And, even if they were willing to listen, they wouldn't have any idea of how to remedy the situation. Behavior-based feedback is impersonal; it doesn't imply character flaws or innate traits. It isn't a value judgment of the recipient as a human being. Rather, it's an assessment of the person's behavior and, as such, is a lot easier for the recipient to accept and act on.

Figure 4.2 suggests behavior-based observations that can be substituted for vague, derogatory labels. When you are delivering feedback to the self-coachee, make sure that you steer clear of the latter.

3. Use the Three-Part Model

One tool that can be very helpful to those providing feedback is the "Three-Part Model": Situation + Behavior + Effect. Phrasing your feedback in this form automatically depersonalizes it. If you were providing feedback to a friend who was always late for your lunch dates, you might say, "Geez, Jerry, you make me crazy because you're always late for lunch and it messes up my whole afternoon." That's a bit incendiary, I'm afraid, and is bound to put Jerry on the defensive.

Using the Three-Part Model instead, you might say something like, "Jerry, the last three times we've had lunch together (situation), you were nearly 20 minutes late (behavior). I didn't get back to campus on time, and I was late for biology lab (effect)." That's much less emotional and far more likely to elicit a promise from Jerry to be on time in the future.

4. Balance Your Feedback

There are four types of feedback:

- **Negative feedback**, or corrective comments about past behavior. These are things that have interfered with the ability to achieve the desired results.

Label	Observed Behavior
1. Is disagreeable	1. Doesn't acknowledge opposing views
2. Is unmotivated	2. Is late for appointments
3. Is stubborn	3. Sticks to his or her views regardless of the facts
4. Is aggressive	4. Yells at those around him or her
5. Is disruptive	5. At family functions, often starts arguments and is intolerant of others' points of view
6. Is lazy	6. Refuses to pitch in and help when needed
7. Is immature	7. Uses humor at inappropriate times
8. Is mature	8. Handles finances responsibly
9. Has poor reasoning power	9. Rushes to judgment without getting all the facts
10. Lacks drive	10. Sets goals but doesn't follow through

FIGURE 4.2 Basing Feedback on Observable Behavior

- **Positive feedback,** or affirming comments about past behavior. These are things that enhanced the ability to achieve the desired results and need to be repeated.
- **Negative feed*forward*,** or corrective comments about future behavior. These are things that should not be repeated as the coachee strives to achieve his or her goals.
- **Positive feed*forward*,** or affirming comments about future behavior. These are things that the coachee can do to increase the likelihood that he or she will reach the goal.[1]

The questionnaire that you are being asked to complete has been designed to gather all four types of feedback. As you are completing it, think about both the past and the future as well as the positive and the negative. Consider the following questions:

- In the past, what behaviors has the self-coachee engaged in that kept him or her from achieving this Intention and/or other Intentions?
- In the past, what behaviors has the self-coachee engaged in that helped in his or her attempts to achieve Intentions?
- What behaviors should the self-coachee avoid engaging in as he or she works toward the fulfillment of this Intention?
- What behaviors should the self-coachee engage in as he or she works toward the fulfillment of this Intention?

When formulating your answers, be sure to include as many positive observations and suggestions as possible without, of course, sugar-coating reality.

As the self-coachee implements his or her plan, you will be asked to assess the progress that has been made and areas in which further work needs to be done. When providing ongoing feedback, make sure that it too is balanced. Many articles and books suggest the following approach: positive feedback/negative feedback/positive feedback. The underlying notion is that "sandwiching" negative feedback between two pieces of positive feedback makes it more palatable and ensures that the person will not tune you out and turn you off.

In theory, this approach works well, but it needs to be carried out carefully. The positive "bread" in the feedback sandwich must be just as specific, observable, and reality-based as the negative "filling." Delivering comforting platitudes is worse than delivering no positive messages because it is sure to undermine the self-coachee's respect for and trust in you.

And, as you see the self-coachee taking forward steps—no matter how small—toward his or her Intention, be sure to acknowledge them and offer your congratulations. In an interesting study of couples conducted at the University of California at Santa Barbara, researchers found that enthusiasm shown by one partner after the other had experienced a positive life event strengthened the relationship even more than support after a negative event. But make sure that your enthusiasm isn't feigned: researchers also found that a passive supportive response, such as saying, "That's nice, honey," then turning back to whatever you're doing is almost as damaging as actually putting down the good event.[2]

5. Suggest, Don't Direct

When making suggestions about future behaviors or actions, try not to be directive. Avoid phrases like, "You must stop smoking right away," or "You can't afford to waste any more time," or "You had better see a doctor." Instead, offer consequence-based suggestions or questions, such as "What do you think is likely to happen if you don't quit smoking this time?" or "Registration for the fall semester will be starting next week. Do you think you should make an appointment to see an advisor this week?"

If possible, suggest an array of options: "You could see your doctor first, then join a support group. What do you think about going for individual counseling?"

6. Be Realistic

When you provide feedback, it needs to be realistic—it needs to take into consideration the person's life situation, interests, intellectual capability, and capacity for self-discipline. If your friend is thinking about majoring in astrophysics, and you know that he can't add a column of numbers, you wouldn't be doing him any favors by endorsing his choice. You could add a lot more value by suggesting that he look at some alternatives before committing to a field that might not play to his strengths.

The self-coachee has chosen you as a supporter because you have a great deal of insight into his or her interests, characteristics, and capabilities. Please keep these in mind when you are formulating your feedback.

7. Don't Hold Back

It's important that you include positive observations, but it's equally vital that you not omit negative ones. The most frustrating, and ultimately unsuccessful, coaching attempts are those in which supporters are reluctant to give the coachee honest, candid feedback.

Criticizing another person's behavior or performance, even if it's done in a constructive spirit, is not easy. We are trained, from early childhood, to "not rock the boat," to "let sleeping dogs lie," and that "If you can't say something nice, don't say anything." We fear that "telling it like it is" will create conflict and cause bad feelings. As a result, in both our business and our personal life, we shy away from raising issues that may damage our relationships with others.

The self-coachee has chosen you as one of his or her supporters because he or she trusts your ability and willingness to be straight with him or her. The self-coachee has given you permission to provide candid feedback on his or her past behavior so that he or she can improve going forward. It's the most valuable gift that you can give, so please don't hold back.

Follow these seven guidelines, and you will become a positive force in the life of someone you care about.

CHAPTER 5

HOW SHOULD YOU RESPOND?

The Self-Coaching Process
1 Determine Your Self-Coachability
2 Select and Commit to an Intention
3 Identify Your Guide and Circle of Support
4 Solicit Feedback
5 Analyze and Respond to Feedback
6 Develop and Act on a Game Plan
7 Track Your Success and Recalibrate

"I just don't see it."

"I don't agree."

"I don't believe it."

"They're mistaken."

"That's not right."

"I never said that."

"I would never do that."

"That's not me."

Denial is sometimes the knee-jerk reaction that I get when I feed back the data from stakeholders to executive coachees. For some of them, this is the first time that anyone has ever held up a mirror to them, and they can't believe what they are seeing. All of a sudden, the portrait hidden in the attic has replaced their idealized image of themselves. How does a coach deal with this disbelief and, often, anger?

A few years ago, I coached a division manager in a large international conglomerate. The feedback from his stakeholders was that he was extremely aggressive and arrogant, didn't listen, and was overbearing. When I shared their comments with him, he became angry and indignant: "How dare they judge me like that? That's a load of bunk!"

After he calmed down a bit, I pointed out that his reaction proved the stakeholders' points. "Doesn't your anger only support what they said about you?" I asked. Taken aback, the executive suddenly realized how accurate a picture his colleagues had painted of him. After this revelation, he began to focus on changing his behavior: soliciting others' opinions, becoming a better listener, and not insisting that it be his way or the highway.

While such a strong initial reaction to feedback is unusual, it does sometimes occur. The initial anger and denial usually dissipate, however, as I go through the Feedback Summary with the coachee. When all the stakeholders agree that the executive needs to dial up his interpersonal skills or when they cite numerous instances in which the person was dismissive or disrespectful of colleagues, it's difficult for the coachee to refute the evidence. The inclusion of positive data—the strengths that the stakeholders attribute to the coachee—cushions the blow and lets the coachee know that there's plenty to draw on to make a change.

I begin every feedback session by encouraging the coachee to depersonalize the data. I tell coachees that at this stage, they need to listen, not react: it's better to be Zenlike than like Attila the Hun. I suggest that to do this, they pretend that the feedback is about someone else, not them.

As a self-coachee, you may very well experience the same surprise when you receive feedback from your Guide and Circle of Support. And you won't have a professional coach to help you put it into perspective. So, in this chapter, I would like to offer some tips to help you handle feedback, analyze it objectively and rationally, and respond to it in a nondefensive, positive way.

LISTENING TO THE MESSAGE

Psychologists tell us that we tend to carry around with us an idealized picture of ourself: an "ego ideal." But, as Theodor Reik has observed, we must also come to terms with a more unsettling counterpicture of ourselves that differs from the ideal.[1] We tend to reject the latter picture and dismiss it out of hand.

You wouldn't be human if you didn't feel some degree of hurt, anger, or dismay when you are told that your behavior doesn't exactly qualify you for canonization: you have failed to keep promises, have been inconsiderate of others, or haven't been living up to your potential. In fact, you may find it even more unsettling because you will not have anyone to guide you through the feedback session. In the personal interviews, you will be sitting alone, face to face, with each member of your Circle as she holds the mirror up to you. As you see yourself, warts and all, reflected in the perceptions of others, it will be up to you to hold your emotions in check, keep telling yourself to depersonalize, and stay neutral.

While I can't be at your side when you receive the feedback, I can offer you some suggestions for how to make an in-person feedback session more rewarding, both for you and for your supporters.

Professional executive coaches are master listeners. They have been trained in active listening and questioning skills, which enable them to put stakeholders at ease and elicit high-value, behavior-based feedback. The following Guidelines for Receiving Feedback are an introduction to some of these key skills and should be top of mind as you gather data from your Guide and your Circle of Support.

GUIDELINES FOR RECEIVING FEEDBACK

If the members of your Circle are willing to give you their feedback in person, try to keep in mind that this experience is as new to them as it is to you. They may be just as apprehensive about commenting on your behavior as you are about hearing their critique. It is up to you to put them at ease and reassure them that you appreciate their candor.

Active listening is the key to successful in-person feedback sessions with the members of your Circle of Support. Active listening is not limited to the ears. It involves the entire body—especially the brain. Following are five effective active-listening techniques that you should employ when you are receiving feedback. Not only will they improve your listening skills, but they will also assure the members of your Circle that you value the messages that they have for you.

1. Attending Behavior

By demonstrating attending behavior, you will convey the message that you are "all ears" and ready to focus completely on what the supporter has to say. It begins with careful selection of the time and place of your meeting. You need ample time, without interruption, at an hour when both of you are fresh and at your best. Don't schedule meetings at the end of a workday—yours or your supporters'. Nor is it a good idea to meet supporters at their place of business, where colleagues can intrude and time can become an issue. If the members of your Circle include members of your immediate family, don't plan to get their feedback at home unless it's at a time when you are alone together. If you can't get the house to yourselves, schedule a leisurely lunch somewhere or, if the weather is good, sit together on a park bench.

Before you begin, reiterate that you are asking for this person's input because you value him and have the utmost respect for his opinion. Stress the fact that you want the person to be candid—to say whatever he wants to without fear of hurting your feelings or making you angry. Tell him again that you will need his ongoing support and will continue to check in with him as you progress toward your goal. And finally, let him know that you see his participation in your Circle of Support as a way of taking your relationship to another level of depth.

Body language speaks volumes, as we all know, and is an important way in which a listener demonstrates attentiveness. Body position, facial expressions, and gestures such as head nodding and hand movements often provide clues to whether you are accepting or rejecting what is being said. Sitting with your arms crossed over your chest, for example, is a body posture that says, "I'm listening, but I'm listening defensively."

I recommend to the executives I coach that they put their stakeholders at ease by adopting the SOLER model of attending behavior, depicted in Figure 5.1.

These nonverbal behaviors have a tremendous impact on the effectiveness of the feedback session. Together with tone of voice—volume, pitch, intensity, and inflection—they are responsible for the lion's share of what people take away from an interaction. In fact, studies have shown that the message retained after an interpersonal exchange is derived 55 percent from nonverbal behavior, 38 percent from tone, and only 7 percent from words.[2]

S – **S**it (or stand) squarely
O – **O**pen posture
L – **L**ean forward
E – **E**ye contact
R – **R**elaxed posture/respect other

FIGURE 5.1 The SOLER Model of Attending Behavior

Creating a private, welcoming environment and adopting a casual, attentive style is the first step in encouraging candid conversation.

2. Passive Listening

Passive listening as an *active* listening skill? It sounds like an oxymoron, but when you stop to think about it, it makes perfect sense. It is possible to remain *passive* while *actively listening.* That doesn't mean that it's easy. Simply remaining silent and allowing the speaker to deliver her message is often a challenge, as our natural inclination is to respond immediately—especially when we believe we have to defend ourselves.

As difficult as it is to maintain, a period of silence is useful because it allows the supporter time to express her thoughts without interruption. During this time, I suggest that you

- Attend to the speaker by simply listening and giving eye contact.
- Observe the speaker's eyes, facial expression, posture, and gestures to glean additional insights.
- Think about what the speaker is saying and feeling.

Such behavior demonstrates, without your having to verbalize, that you are completely receptive to your supporter's message.

3. "Say More" Responses

"Say more" responses are questions and comments that encourage the speaker to tell you more about his ideas and feelings or to clarify them for you. They can be neutral statements, such as "Really," "Uh, huh," and "Oh?" or more direct invitations to continue, such as "Tell me more" or "Go ahead." If you need more clarification, you may ask, "Can you explain?" or "Can you give me an example?"

Say more responses are a very effective way of keeping the members of your Circle focused on the *specific, behavior-based feedback* that you need if you are to begin to make the changes that will advance you toward your Intention. These responses should not communicate any of your own judgments, thoughts, or feelings. Rather, they are meant to let the speaker know that you are putting yourself in his shoes to better understand his perception of you.

4. Paraphrasing

Paraphrasing means repeating back to the speaker, in your own words, your understanding of what she has told you. *Mirroring* is another word for this technique, which eliminates the potential for misunderstanding.

When you are paraphrasing, focus on the *content* of the message, not the emotion behind it. Try to capture, as concisely as possible, exactly what the supporter has said. Then, ask him to confirm that your interpretation of the message is correct.

Here are some formulations that you can use when paraphrasing:

"It sounds like . . ."

"So, what you are saying is . . ."

"It seems to me that you . . ."

"Let me see if I understand you correctly . . ."

"When you say __________, do you mean ___________?"

5. Decoding and Feeding Back Feelings

Once you understand the *what* of the message, it is time to search for the *why*. This is often difficult to do because, when people speak to one another, especially about emotionally charged or highly personal issues, they often encode the message rather than letting it all hang out. Even though you have given the members of your Circle permission to be candid with you, some of them may be reluctant to tell "the whole truth and nothing but the truth." This becomes even more likely when your Intention is to stop some type of destructive or self-destructive behavior, such as alcohol or drug abuse, gambling, or violent outbursts.

Figure 5.2 illustrates how people encode messages and the resultant decoding that we often have to do.

The diagram shows the speaker sending—or encoding—a message to the listener. The speaker encodes her thoughts and feelings into a verbal message, and the listener, in turn, decodes the message by reflecting back the thoughts and feelings that he believes the speaker is sharing. Unfortunately, filters can prevent the speaker from delivering the message clearly and concisely. Age, gender, cultural differences, educational differences, and belief

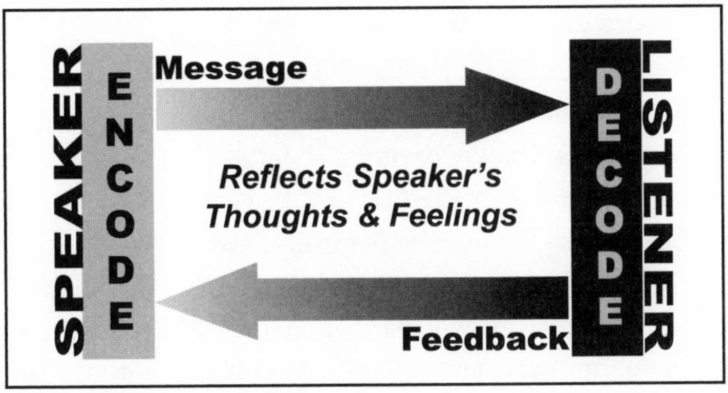

FIGURE 5.2 Decoding a Speaker's Message and Feeding It Back

systems are common filters. Also, speakers often disguise their real messages or use words inappropriately for fear of hurting others. As a result, the listener may be able to decode the message only partially.

To complicate the process further, just as the speaker may encode inaccurately, the listener—in this case, you—may decode inaccurately as a result of his own filtering system.

As with paraphrasing, the goal of decoding and feeding back is to communicate to your supporters your understanding of the subtext of their messages and your acceptance of their reality. By providing them with a restatement or reworking of the emotional message, you indicate whether or not you "got it." If the restatements are accurate, your supporters will be encouraged to go on. If not, they will receive the signal that they need to clarify the message so that you can receive it more accurately.

When a person transmits a message about emotions, what is *not* spoken sometimes reveals more than what is put into words. True feelings are often revealed more by a gesture, a facial expression, or the tone or volume of voice than by the words. When decoding, then, it is important that you be receptive to both verbal and nonverbal clues.

The following statements are examples of phrases that you can use when feeding back to your supporters the emotions that you have decoded during your active listening:

"When I do __________, it seems to *annoy* you."

"You seem *frustrated*."

"It sounds as if you're *confused* about . . ."

"You're *nervous*."

"I believe you are *angry* with me because . . ."

Remember, the closer your relationship with the supporter, the more likely it is that she will react emotionally and will try to couch that emotion in "acceptable" terms. As difficult as it may be, you will need to keep probing until you've gotten all the issues out into the open.

Make sure that you take careful, comprehensive notes during the interview. You may want to ask each person's permission to record the session so that you can share it with your Guide during the analysis step.

At the end of each interview, thank the person and make sure that you tell her that you and your Guide will be analyzing the data from all the members of your Circle. Explain that the two of you will construct a plan based on their input, and you will get back to each member of your Circle. Make sure you schedule these follow-up interviews as soon as possible after receiving the feedback.

When Receiving Feedback . . .

- **Keep in mind that this is how you are perceived.**
- **Keep an open mind; your supporter may be right.**
- **Don't get defensive.**
- **Hear the entire message, then test to make sure you've understood it.**
- **Thank your supporter for the feedback.**

ANALYZING THE DATA

As an executive coach, one of my duties is to analyze the feedback from the stakeholders and present it to the coachee. What has been said, how it was said, and what was meant must all be considered. As Figure 4.1 in the previous chapter shows, as a self-coachee, you and your Guide will share this task, reviewing and discussing the feedback that you've received from your Circle of Support. (If you ask your supporters to submit their feedback online, Guttman Development Strategies will consolidate the survey answers for you, but analyzing them will still be the responsibility of you and your Guide.)

The object of the analysis is to identify major themes or issues that recur in most or all of the responses. The themes may relate to behaviors that the self-coachee needs to eliminate or to new behaviors to replace the old, limiting ones. When dealing with personal Intentions, self-coachees are likely to hear these or similar themes:

- Unless you thicken your skin and learn to deal with rejection, you're not going to succeed in sales.
- You tend to lose enthusiasm about a month into every new project or interest.
- You won't be able to stop drinking as long as you keep running with your present crowd.
- You often turn to food for comfort when you are bored or lonely.
- You tend to overpromise and underdeliver.
- You need to improve your use of the English language if you want a career in broadcast journalism.
- You are very creative, but you don't have the discipline to translate your ideas into reality.
- Your family takes advantage of you; you need to learn to say no and mean it.
- You have a great sense of humor; you should try to use it to your advantage.

When you and your Guide analyze the data, look for themes and their implications. In order to qualify as a theme, the same comment must be made by a significant number of stakeholders (assuming that your Circle is made up of more than two or three people). Let's say that there are eight people in your Circle of Support, and one of them provided you with the feedback that "You tend to overpromise and underdeliver." There are a number of questions that you and your Guide might want to probe as you assess this feedback: How many others provided you with similar feedback? Did others offer similar examples of overpromising and underdelivering? Is there a pattern? For example, have you been observed overpromising at certain times and in certain situations and not in others? Are there any distinctions between the times when you overpromised and those when you did not? Does this reveal possible causes that you can try to correct?

During the analysis, you'll be looking for themes in the responses to each of the questions. What areas do the majority of your supporters say you need to develop? What do most of them think are your strengths? What actions were most frequently recommended to help you move toward your Intention? What barriers or challenges do your supporters agree are likely to derail you?

If you have been able to tape the individual interviews, listening to them with your Guide may prove even more valuable than just sharing your written notes. Not only will he be able to help you identify themes, but hearing the interaction between you and each supporter—intonation, choice of words, moments of hesitation, enthusiasm or lack thereof—can give your Guide additional insights into unspoken or encoded messages and underlying emotions.

CONSTRUCTING THE PLAN

Once you and your Guide have analyzed the data and identified the major themes and issues, you can begin to construct a *Personal Development Plan (PDP)*. This will include actions to move you toward your Intention; a time line, which should be as specific as possible; a list of potential problems or barriers to the achievement of your Intention; and a list of actions that you can take now and in the future to break through these barriers.

During this step, the Guide acts as a sort of "shadow coach." Like an executive coach, she helps the self-coachee to come up with his own solutions rather than providing the answers.

In Chapter 6, we will discuss planning in detail.

CLOSING THE LOOP

If you look back at Figure 4.1 in Chapter 4, you will notice that in both executive and self-coaching, "Closing the Loop" is primarily the responsibility of the person who is being coached.

I prepare the executives I coach by providing them with a *Discussion Plan* for this step. We fill in the plan data together, and the coachee then uses it to guide the meeting with each stakeholder.

The Discussion Plan covers the following points:

1. Expression of gratitude for the feedback.
2. Sharing of headlines or key issues from the feedback analysis: *"Here's what I heard about my strengths and areas for development."*
3. Sharing of the Personal Development Plan (see Chapter 6 for a discussion of the planning process): *"Here's what I plan to do."*
4. Identification of additional issues and new agreements: *"Are there any other issues between you and me that we need to clear up?" "Is there anything that I've missed?"*
5. Request for ongoing feedback and support: *"I'm always willing to listen; give me feedback anytime." "May I get back to you to test my progress?"*

Now let's return to Steve, whose Feedback Summary appeared at the beginning of Chapter 4. After analyzing his feedback, he and I created the following Discussion Plan for him to follow when closing the loop with his stakeholders.

ORGANIZATIONAL STRATEGY AND ALIGNMENT

1. Thank you for your participation.
2. Some key messages I heard were:

   My strengths:

   - Strong HR expertise

- Calmness under fire
- Ability to see the big picture and utilize the appropriate organizational resources to address issues or problems
- Good communication/people skills

Developmental opportunities for me:

- Strengthen my leadership presence, influencing ability, and assertiveness
- Interact effectively with the different cultures within the region
- Become a collaborative business partner with the country stakeholders and GMs in the region
- Effectively manage the relationship with the head of the corporate HR department
- Build a strong HR team within the region

3. What I am planning to do is:
   - Meet with all those who provided feedback to establish actions for moving forward in building strong collaborative business partnerships with them
   - Work with the executive coach to raise my level of assertiveness, influencing skills, and leadership presence
   - Create a Game Plan to raise my level of cultural awareness in the region, including establishing an ongoing communication/feedback loop with my predecessor
   - Formulate specific Game Plans for clearly communicating expectations to my staff and for raising the skill level of my team
   - Establish a follow-up communication plan with the head of the corporate HR department

4. Are there any other issues between you and me that need to be resolved? What actions can I take to help resolve them?

Write down any new agreement(s).

5. I would appreciate any further input from you going forward . . .

Now go to Action Step 5.1 and create your own Discussion Plan.

At this point, the actual coaching or self-coaching begins, as the executive and coach or self-coachee and Guide begin to implement the plan. We'll talk about implementation in Chapter 7, but before we approach that subject, we need to provide some guidance on developing a plan, or "Mapping Your Route," which we will do in Chapter 6.

Action Step 5.1: Creating Your Discussion Plan

Working with your Guide, create your own Discussion Plan for the follow-up meetings that you will hold with your Circle of Support. Write your plan on a separate sheet of paper or enter it on the form you downloaded from www.coachyourselftowin.com. Include:

1. An expression of gratitude for the feedback:
2. Sharing of headlines or key issues from the feedback analysis:
   - Here's what I heard about my strengths
   - Here's what I heard about the areas in which I need development
3. Sharing of your Personal Development Plan (to be completed after reading Chapter 6)
   - Here are some of the things I plan to do, and the dates by which I will have done them
4. Identification of additional issues and new agreements:
   - Is there anything else that needs to be resolved between you and me? Is there anything I've missed?
5. Request for ongoing feedback and support
   - Please feel free to give me additional feedback at any time.
   - May I get back to you to test my progress?

After the coachee has closed the loop with three or so stakeholders, I talk to her to see how it has been going and whether or not any new data points have come up that may necessitate changes or additions to the plan. I suggest that you and your Guide follow the same procedure after you've conducted a few follow-up meetings.

CHAPTER 6

MAPPING YOUR ROUTE

The Self-Coaching Process
1 Determine Your Self-Coachability
2 Select and Commit to an Intention
3 Identify Your Guide and Circle of Support
4 Solicit Feedback
5 Analyze and Respond to Feedback
6 Develop and Act on a Game Plan
7 Track Your Success and Recalibrate

PERSONAL TRANSFORMATION

> In a field one summer's day a Grasshopper was hopping about, chirping and singing to its heart's content. An Ant walked by, grunting as he carried a plump kernel of corn.
>
> "Where are you off to with that heavy thing?" asked the Grasshopper.
>
> Without stopping, the Ant replied, "To our ant hill. This is the third kernel I've delivered today."
>
> "Why not come and sing with me," said the Grasshopper, "instead of working so hard?"
>
> "I am helping to store food for the winter," said the Ant, "and think you should do the same."
>
> "Why bother about winter?" said the Grasshopper; "we have plenty of food right now."
>
> But the Ant went on its way and continued its work.
>
> The weather soon turned cold. All the food lying in the field was covered with a thick white blanket of snow that even the Grasshopper could not dig through. Soon the Grasshopper found itself dying of hunger.
>
> He staggered to the Ants' hill and saw them handing out corn from the stores they had collected in the summer . . .[1]

Do you always save room for dessert? Take an umbrella when there's a 50-50 change of rain? Buy toilet paper in the 24-pack? If so, you're cut from the same cloth as Aesop's ant: always thinking ahead and making sure that you are prepared for every eventuality. You're going to have no trouble absorbing and implementing the ideas in this chapter.

But what if you're more like the grasshopper: content to take life one day at a time, enjoying the moment instead of focusing on the future? If that describes you, internalizing the concepts presented here is going to be something of a challenge.

The idea of sitting down and writing out a detailed plan might seem quite alien to you at first. I can hear you asking: "How can I possibly think that far ahead? How do I know what's going to happen next week or next month, much less what to do about it?"

My answer: planning isn't so much about predicting the future as it is about trying to shape it. Think about it. *The* future doesn't really exist; there are only *possible futures*. By planning carefully now, you at least increase the odds that, of all the possible futures, the one that you actually desire will be most likely to materialize.

We all know that the future is not predictable, at least not scientifically. How can it be, when there are no future facts? But we can look back at the past and reflect upon the present to examine behavior—ours as well as others'—and make judgments about what is or is not likely to work as we move ahead into the unknown. Here, the voice of experience can be a powerful ally, especially when we might have previously failed or fallen short of realizing our Intention. Bad experience often makes for good planning.

I'm not going to pretend that planning is a cakewalk. On the contrary, developing your plan is going to require deep thinking and lots of creativity. But I guarantee that putting in this extra effort up front will spare you many setbacks and regrets later on. No matter what your Intention, whether you are being coached by a professional or following this self-coaching process, *failing to plan is planning to fail.*

I don't believe that we are born either grasshoppers or ants. We become one or the other based on our life experience. In Chapter 2, we discussed the fact that the "stories" we tell ourselves about our ability to reach our Intentions are rooted in influences and events from our past. We also create stories, based on past experience, about our ability to plan ahead.

Here are a number of stories that people commonly tell themselves to rationalize their failure to plan.

Stories That Kill Planning

- It's too complicated.
- I run on instinct.
- I'd rather live in the moment.
- I can't be that specific.
- I'm not the federal government. Why do I need to plan?
- Remember what they say about "the best-laid plans of mice and men."
- I'd rather *do* than plan.
- I don't have the time.
- *Que serà, serà.*
- I don't know where to start.
- I'll get started tomorrow.
- Don't worry, be happy.

Do you hide behind any of these stories in order to avoid making concrete plans to improve your personal or professional life? Do you have any other stories about why you became a grasshopper instead of an ant? Such stories can suck the oxygen out of your Intention. Surely, one of the best tests for determining the strength of your Intention is whether or not you back up your Intention with a plan.

Let's flip to Action Step 6.1 at the end of the chapter and take a quick reality test of the stories about planning that you may be holding. As you do, refer back to the discussion in Chapter 2 on how to move from stories that hold you back to ones that propel you ahead, toward your Intention.

Once you've completed Action Step 6.1, congratulations are in order—your transformation has begun! But before you rush out to gather those kernels, I'd like to say a little bit about the principles on which all good plans are based.

PLANNING PILLARS

Planning is your bridge to the future. As you think about how to build that bridge, let me share with you 10 pillars upon which to build your plan.

1. **Be Intention-focused**. It goes without saying that your Intention is the mother lode of your plan; everything in your plan must be directed toward reaching it. Ask, "As I begin to develop my plan, what are the key elements that must be in place if I am to accomplish my Intention?"
2. **Be realistic.** "A man's reach should exceed his grasp, or what's a heaven for?" Robert Browning's line makes for good poetry but poor planning. A plan that doesn't put your Intention safely within your grasp should be scrapped. In fact, the first test of the realism of your plan is your response to this question: "Will this plan deliver me to my Intention?" Next, ask: "Are the time lines in the plan realistic? What about the steps that I have laid out and the resources I will need to accomplish them?"
3. **Avoid complexity**. A professor of political science at Notre Dame used to caution graduate students who were about to embark on writing a dissertation that, "There are two kinds of dissertations: the great works and those that get written." You can say the same thing about plans. You can build plans that resemble Gothic cathedrals of grandeur and intricacy, with all the latest accoutrements, such as Gantt charts and critical paths, or you can follow the KISS mode: keep it simple, stupid. There is no need to get fancy. Just get the job done.

5. **Build in "what-ifs."** Franz Kafka, the great existentialist writer, once observed, "In a fight between you and the world, back the world." His rather gloomy statement is a variation on

Murphy's Law: whatever can go wrong, will. While we don't advise brooding pessimism, it's best to go into planning with your eyes wide open, knowing that even the best-laid plans have a way of going awry. We live in a world in which chance rules. Every good plan must grapple with the question: "What actions can I take if things don't go according to plan?"

5. **Set time lines.** I was talking recently to a retired military officer who had decided to buy a camp in a remote area of Tennessee. His aim was to provide an artistic venue for aspiring actors and producers, and at the same time stimulate the local economy. His goal was certainly a noble one, but when I asked the former officer about his time frame for reaching it, he hemmed and hawed. I asked, "When will you have your first actors on site? When do you plan to connect with producers and writers? When do you see yourself breaking even? And when will your Intention be fully implemented?" He had no answers. There were plenty of "whats" in his thinking, but few "whens." The fewer the "whens" and the more the "whenevers," the greater the likelihood that "never ever" will be the outcome.

   Time lines for actions hold your feet to the fire. They impose discipline. Without them, your plans are likely to become pie in the sky.

6. **Cover all the bases.** Good planning, whether in business or in your personal life, involves using a systematic process. Such a process ensures that you cover all the bases. What are they? As you will soon see, they involve identifying the sequence of steps and substeps necessary to implement your plan, setting a range of actions that must be in place, and then laying out the time frames and responsibilities for moving ahead. When you've completed your plan, step back and ask: "If I were to do what I've set forth in the order and time frame outlined, would my Intention become reality?"

7. **Deconstruct it**. We know a management trainer who teaches seminar participants how to break problems apart, into discrete subproblems. "How do you eat an elephant?" he likes to ask his students. His answer: "One bite at a time." As you go through each step in your plan, break it down into discrete, bite-sized chunks. You'll find it much easier to swallow!

   Anecdotal evidence aside, research confirms that small is good. In his classic article "Small Wins," organizational theorist Karl Weick demonstrates that when an obstacle appears to be too big, complex, or difficult, people become overwhelmed and freeze. Break down the same challenge and people proceed with confidence to overcome it.[2]

8. **Write it down.** Psychologists tell us that the human brain can handle only from five to seven elements or "chunks" of data simultaneously. And those of us who have advanced beyond the 50-yard line in life know that even five such elements can be a stretch. If you don't write down your plan, be prepared to write it off.

9. **Test your thinking**. "Am I being realistic? What have I left out? Is there a better way?" Bring your Guide and your Circle of Support into the planning mix. Let them take a good, hard look at your plan. Being up close and personal can lead to myopia. A fresh pair of eyes reduces the blind spots.

10. **Be resilient.** "To bounce without breaking" is the best way to deal with risk, according to Aaron Wildavsky's classic work on the subject, *Searching for Safety*.[3] Even if you can't predict the future, and even if the contingencies you have built into your plan don't work out—in other words, if you fall back in your progress toward your Intention—the trick is to repair, recover, and redirect yourself. Keep bouncing back to your Intention.

Because many people are put off by the idea of creating a detailed plan, we have created a simple, straightforward process that doesn't require an advanced degree. It's based on these 10 pillars, along with your common sense and experience.

In the pages that follow, we'll discuss a plan that incorporates these elements and show you a completed plan. Then you'll work with your Guide to create your Personal Development Plan, or PDP. Additional plans and a blank template are available on www.coachyourselftowin.com.

As we have in previous chapters, let's begin by looking at the differences and similarities between the executive-coaching and self-coaching models.

HOLDING THE PLANNING MEETING

If you look back at Figure 4.1 in Chapter 4, which outlines the responsibilities in the process for soliciting feedback and responding to it, you'll see that Step 4 of both models, "Constructing the Plan," is a collaborative effort: between the coach and the coachee in executive coaching, and between the Guide and the self-coachee in self-coaching.

In each case, it's up to the person who is serving as a consultant to make sure that the following agenda items are covered in the planning meeting with the coachee or self-coachee:

1. Based on the feedback, set objectives for the plan. (Use SMART criteria: specific, measurable, achievable, realistic, and time-bounded.)
2. For each objective, list the steps, or actions, that will be taken to achieve it.
3. For each action, list the measures or evidence that will be used to assess success.

4. For each action, identify the target date for completion and identify who needs to be involved.
5. Set dates when progress on the plan will be assessed and adjustments made.

I have already described how I present the Feedback Summary to the executives I coach, asking them to depersonalize, control their emotions, ask only clarifying questions, and look for trends. When I feel that the individual understands and accepts the feedback, we are ready to begin planning.

At the start of the planning meeting, I once again ask the coachee to depersonalize. "Let's pretend that you and I are both consultants," I say. "We are being paid to figure out, together, the best way to get this person to reach his Intention."

I explain that our purpose is to suggest the most effective actions the person can take to show up differently. Our suggestions can't be philosophical or academic in nature. We can't just offer generalities and leave it at that. Whatever actions we recommend must be descriptive, specific, realistic, and directed toward behaviors that can be changed.

As an experienced executive coach, I have conducted many planning meetings, but for your Guide this might be a first. Since in this meeting she is acting as a "shadow coach," later in this chapter I have provided some "Dos and Don'ts for Guides." This is the same advice that we give to consultants and human resources professionals who are starting out in executive coaching. It is designed to help new coaches or Guides set the right tone for the planning meeting and ensure that the plan that they create is truly a collaborative effort between them and the coachee or self-coachee.

Please make sure that your Guide has an opportunity to review these dos and don'ts before you sit down with him to develop your plan. In fact, I highly recommend that if your Guide hasn't read this book yet, he at least read this chapter before you sit down together to develop your plan.

DEVELOPING THE PLAN: SETTING "SMART" OBJECTIVES

Whether you are being coached or coaching yourself, the first step in developing your plan is setting objectives. The executive coach and coachee or the Guide and self-coachee begin the process by looking at the themes that were spotted in the stakeholder feedback. To illustrate how this plays out in the executive-coaching model, let's go back to our old friend Steve, who had set the Intention to successfully perform his job duties in the Asia/Pacific Region.

When Steve and I sat down to discuss his stakeholders' feedback, we identified the following development opportunities that had been suggested for him:

1. Strengthen his leadership presence, influencing ability, and assertiveness
2. Interact effectively with the different cultures within the region
3. Become a collaborative business partner with the country stakeholders and GMs in the region
4. Manage the relationship with the head of the corporate HR department effectively
5. Build a strong HR team within the region

Each of these was actually an objective that his stakeholders believed Steve needed to achieve in order to be successful in his new position. But, like most objectives suggested during the feedback process, these were too broad to be actionable. It was up to Steve and me to break them down into SMART goals, then design actions to help him achieve each.

Many people with a business background are familiar with the acronym SMART, which is often used when setting goals for projects, individual or team performance, and business outcomes.

If you haven't heard the term before, SMART goals are

S = SPECIFIC

They focus on a particular situation and define specific actions or tasks

Not specific: *Learn more about leadership this month.*

Specific: *Read the three bestselling books on leadership this month.*

M = MEASURABLE

They include specific levels of accomplishment and ways to let you know when the objective has been reached.

Not measureable: *Increase the number of push-ups I can do over the course of the next six months.*

Measurable: *Increase the number of push-ups I do to 50 per day over the course of the next six months.*

A = ACHIEVABLE

They are reasonable accomplishments; they require a degree of stretch, but they are not entirely out of reach.

Not achievable: *Achieve a 100 percent success rate on sales calls this quarter.*

Achievable: *Increase my successful sales calls by 10 percent this quarter.*

R = REALISTIC

They are within the realm of possibility, rooted in reality; they are not "pie in the sky" wishes.

Unrealistic: *Become a world-renowned concert pianist by next summer.*

Realistic: *Learn to play the piano well enough to get a job in a local lounge next summer.*

T = TIME BOUNDED

They are achievable within a specified period of time.

Not time-bounded: *Run a marathon someday.*

Time-bounded: *Run in the American Heart Association marathon taking place next April.*[4]

To ensure that your objectives meet the SMART criteria, I suggest that, when writing them down, you include three components:

- Responsibility statement: *What has to be done?*
- Performance measure: *How much/how well? (quality/quantity/cost)*
- Time orientation: *By when?*

A simple format that includes these components is as follows:

______________ +	______________ +	______________
Action Verb (What?)	*Performance Measure (How much/How well?)*	*Time Orientation (By when?)*

Since objectives are results to be achieved, begin writing them with an action verb: increase, decrease, reduce, complete, prepare, compile. Using verbs such as understand, learn, or gain knowledge of will give you not-so-SMART objectives that cannot be measured. You can measure only what you see a person do with her understanding or knowledge—i.e., behavior change.

For example, you cannot measure whether a customer service rep "Understands the components of good customer service." You can measure only the outcomes that demonstrate understanding, such as "Achieves a customer satisfaction rating of X percent each month." Likewise, it's meaningless to say, "Improve my health." There needs to be some measure of improvement, such as "Get my blood pressure down consistently to 120 over 80" or "Lower my cholesterol by 70 points."

Test your understanding of SMART objectives by flipping to Action Step 6.2 at the end of the chapter and rewriting the broad objectives given there, using the format just described.

SMART OBJECTIVES IN ACTION

Getting back to Steve, he and I took each of the five broad objectives suggested in the feedback and broke it down into a number of SMART objectives. For example:

Strengthen His Leadership Presence, Influencing Ability, and Assertiveness

We began by discussing what Steve's stakeholders meant when they referred to his "leadership presence." We concluded that having leadership presence means coming across as a powerful person, someone who exudes confidence and competence, is obviously in control of himself and the situation, and commands respect. A leader shouldn't be viewed as aggressive or unapproachable, but he should definitely be considered a "force to be reckoned with."

Next, we looked at the traits that are associated with successfully influencing others, especially those over whom you don't have direct control. Here, because of my long career in skill building, I was able to provide Steve with a lot of useful insights. If you want to be able to influence others, you need to listen actively, collaborate, and manage conflict so that it's a win-win for all involved. He agreed that these were skills that he needed to hone.

Third, we needed to decide how Steve could show up as neither nonassertive nor aggressive, but sufficiently assertive to get his points of view across without alienating others.

Engaging in these clarifying conversations enabled us to come up with the following SMART objectives for Steve:

- In my professional interactions, show up as a leader who is confident, competent, and approachable.
- Improve my skills in the following areas: active listening, collaboration, and conflict management.
- On the continuum of behavior from nonassertive to assertive to aggressive, move to the middle in my professional interactions.

You have probably noticed that I haven't included time frames in these objectives. Most executive coaching requires a commitment of between 9 and 12 months, and that is the overall time frame that we set for Steve to achieve all his objectives and arrive at his Intention. Once we began planning actions to meet these objectives, we set shorter time frames to accomplish each action. For example, I asked Steve to study the grooming and dress habits of high-profile executives before our first scheduled coaching session. When you set your personal objectives, you'll need to make sure that they, and the actions related to each, are time-bounded.

Interact Effectively with the Different Cultures within the Region

Meeting this second broad objective was critical for Steve. As you'll recall, when he first began working in the Asia/Pacific Region, his colleagues were quite concerned about his U.S.-centric view of the world. We had to come up with a game plan that would shift Steve's view of the universe and others' perception of him.

SMART objectives that needed to be accomplished were:

- Learn as much as possible about Asian culture, traditions, acceptable and unacceptable behaviors and language, business protocols, and social conventions, especially those of Japan, where I am going to be based.
- Replace the stories about Asian/Japanese people and culture that have kept me from interacting effectively with them.
- Learn from the experience of others who have worked in the region.

We followed the same process for the three other broad objectives that had been suggested for Steve.

PLANNING ACTIONS

Once we had a comprehensive list of SMART objectives, Steve and I brainstormed to come up with the most effective actions he could take to accomplish each. As coach, I kept in mind that this was, first and foremost, *Steve's* plan. In order for it to work, he had to be 100 percent invested in it. I encouraged him to come up with actions; questioned him to make sure that he was aware of the positive and negative consequences of those actions; and, when I had questions about the effectiveness of his suggestions, offered other options for his consideration.

For each action, we decided how to measure whether or not Steve had successfully accomplished it, set a target date for its completion, and wrote down the names of any other people who needed to be involved. Finally, we set dates when progress on the plan would be assessed and adjustments made. As the plan was implemented, progress toward completing each action was recorded in a "Status" column.

We recorded all this information on Steve's Personal Development Plan. Each executive that we coach has a PDP, which is completed with her coach. The amount of detail in each plan will vary, depending on the extent of the coaching required. But having the plan set down in black and white and in one document, goes a long way toward ensuring that it will be carried out in a methodical, timely fashion.

The portion of Steve's PDP that relates to his second broad objective can be viewed on www.coachyourselftowin.com, along with more examples of PDPs that have been created for the executives we coach.

A WORD ABOUT WATCH-OUTS

As a self-coachee, you are going to be following the same planning process that we use in executive coaching. You will be completing a Personal Development Plan template just like Steve's, with one exception.

Executive coaching takes place in a very structured environment where as little as possible is left to chance. It's like driving on a closed course in automobile racing: there are no potholes, no downed trees across the road, no "construction ahead" or "detour" signs. It's pretty much a straight shot in that, from the outset, we make certain that the coachee is going to be given all the resources that he needs to make the coaching a success. It is clearly understood by the executive's boss and colleagues that the coaching sessions are going to be held on a regular schedule and will take precedence over anything else except emergencies. And, as coach, I am always watching out for roadblocks and barriers that might slow us down or get us off track.

Your journey, on the other hand, is going to be taking you through the equivalent of city streets, where you get stuck at red lights and pedestrians leap out from between parked cars. You are much more likely to run into roadblocks, detours, and gridlock than someone who is being coached by a professional would be. When your Guide is in the passenger seat, she will be able to point out hazards and help you navigate through them. But much of the time you'll be driving solo, and you'll have to stay alert at all times.

That's why we include a couple of additional elements in the Personal Development Plan for self-coachees: *watch-outs, or possible barriers to success,* and *ways to get around them.*

When you asked your Guide and Circle of Support for feedback, one of the questions you put to them was, "What two to three things should be the greatest 'watch-outs' for me—the things that are most likely to cause me to derail?" Their answers will be the starting point for your planning in this area.

Let's say that your Intention is to lose 20 pounds in the next six months, and several members of your Circle said that they have often seen you turn to food for comfort when you were bored or lonely. With this feedback in mind, you can begin to plan strategies for dealing with boredom and loneliness *before they set in.* You might make a list of local sights that you've always wanted to see but never got around to. If you're bored on a Sunday afternoon, consult your list, hop in the car or on a bus, and visit one of the sights instead of spending the day snacking in front of the TV. Or lay in a stash of videos—some that you've seen and loved and some that you've been wanting to view but haven't had time for. Turn on the DVD player and enjoy an evening of long-anticipated entertainment. Invite a friend to join you if you need added support to keep you from breaking out the popcorn.

Don't rely on your Circle, however, to point out all the dangers. Take off the blinders and take a long, honest look at your behavior and habits. If you have been trying to give up gambling, but every time you see your brother-in-law, he's taking bets on a game, and you can't resist trying your luck, that's a watch-out. Meeting with him puts your Intention at risk, and you've got to build into your plan a way to either avoid him entirely or keep from succumbing to temptation when he's around. The following solution may be extreme, but it works for an acquaintance of mine. She imagines that her cousin, a binge eater, has a yellow Post-it stuck to her forehead that says, "I'm toxic." This is my friend's way of holding fast to her Intention of losing 30 pounds by keeping her guard up whenever that cousin is around.

CREATING YOUR PERSONAL DEVELOPMENT PLAN

Before you begin working on your own PDP, let's discuss a typical plan made by a self-coachee.

Keely J. already has a bachelor's degree in English. Her Guide is her former college roommate, Linda K. The two graduated four years ago. With her degree in English, Keely quickly got a job as an editor at a large publishing house, but she no longer finds the work meaningful. She has been volunteering at a hospital for the last two years, and she finds great satisfaction in helping patients. She has observed the registered nurses at work, and she has decided that she would be very happy and fulfilled if she were an RN herself. She has set an Intention to be working as a registered nurse within three years. She asked her Circle of Support, which, besides Linda, includes two nurses from the hospital where she volunteers and her sister, to assess her strengths and areas for development and to point out some of the challenges that she may have to face. Keely and Linda sat down together and drew up the plan for Keely's career transition that appears on pages 174–177.

Because they were dealing with a long-range plan that wouldn't be completed for three years, Keely and Linda focused most of their attention on the first broad objective: Keely's need to get a nursing degree. Keely will obviously continue to think about the next phases in her three-year plan, but at this point there are a limited number of actions that she can take to get her closer to her goal. Once she is a few months from graduation, she can go back to the remaining sections of this plan and begin adding detail.

Now that you have seen how a PDP is completed, it's time to create one to reach *your* Intention. Go to Action Step 6.3 to begin developing your PDP.

COMMUNICATING YOUR PROGRESS

At the end of your planning meeting, you are ready to begin implementing your PDP. First, however, you need to communicate what you have done so far to your Circle of Support.

As I explained in Chapter 5, in my executive coaching I prepare my coachees to go back to each of their stakeholders and summarize what they have decided to do and when. There's no need to go through each line of the plan; an overview will suffice in most cases.

In Chapter 5, I showed you the summary that Steve personally presented to his stakeholders regarding the plans that we made to ensure that he was successful in his new position. Here it is again:

What I am planning to do is

- Meet with all those who provided feedback to establish actions for moving forward in building strong collaborative business partnerships with them
- Work with the executive coach to raise my level of assertiveness, influencing skills, and leadership presence
- Create a game plan to raise my level of cultural awareness in the region, including establishing an ongoing communication/feedback loop with my predecessor
- Formulate specific game plans for clearly communicating expectations to my staff and for raising the skill level of my team

Self-coachee: Keely J.

Overall Goal/Intention: Be employed as a registered nurse within three years

Guide: Linda K.

Date of Plan: 1/1/2010

Target Completion Date: 1/1/2013

Broad and SMART Objectives	Actions	Target Date	Involvement of Others	
I. Get my two-year nursing degree		6/2012		
a. Find out requirements: prior education, cost, dates when applications are due, and so on	1. Meet with admissions officers at local schools that offer nursing degree (three in area)	1/15/10		
b. Select a school	1 Compare programs (cost, curriculum, quality of faculty, and so on)	1/22/10		
	2. Speak to graduates of each school	1/31/10	At least two grads from each school	
	3. Rank first, second, and third choices	2/1/10		
c. Get financial aid	1. During initial meetings with admissions, ask about available aid, eligibility requirements, deadlines, and so on	1/15/10		
	2. Submit aid applications, with all supporting documents	3/1/10		
d. Apply to all three schools	1. Submit applications, with all supporting documents	3/1/10		

	Watch-Outs/ Possible Barriers to Success	Ways to Overcome Barriers	Measures/ Evidence	Status
	Schools may be on winter break	Call immediately and set up appointments as soon as break ends	Appointments made	
	I don't know enough RNs personally	Ask schools to arrange for me to speak with grads		
			Ranking done	
	Not enough aid available	Investigate other sources of financing Rethink plan	Information obtained	
	Don't have all required information by the deadlines	Start getting information together ASAP	Aid applications filed by deadline	
	Don't have all required information by deadlines	Start getting information together ASAP; identify extra references in case I can't contact first choices; pick up transcripts in person rather than having schools mail them to me	Applications filed by deadline	

Broad and SMART Objectives	Actions	Target Date	Involvement of Others	
II. Pass RN licensing exam		9/20/12		
a. Find out where and when next licensing exam is being given	1. Contact State Examination Dept. to get dates and locations	5/12		
b. Thoroughly prepare for exam	1. Take a preparatory course	6/12	Company that offers courses	
c. Take exam		9/12		
III. Get a job as an RN		1/2013		
a. Find out what jobs are available in my area	1. Sign up at nursing school's placement office	6/12		
	2. Subscribe to publications for nurses that advertise positions	6/12		
	3. Network at hospital where I volunteer	6/12	Hospital employee	
b. Apply for positions that are of most interest to me	1. Prepare my résumé and cover letter	9/12		
	2. Have professional résumé-writer review résumé and letter	9/12	Professional writer	
	3. Line up references	9/12	Possible references	
c. Interview and get job offer		By 1/13		

	Watch-Outs/ Possible Barriers to Success	Ways to Overcome Barriers	Measures/ Evidence	Status
			Information obtained	
	Course not being given in my area at this time	Find out where course is being given and arrange to take it there	Course passed	
			Exam passed	
	No suitable jobs in my area	Expand my search to other parts of the state	Identify at least three available jobs that interest me	
	References can't be located or don't want to be contacted	Have list of alternates in case first choices fall out	Résumés and cover letters submitted	
			I've got a job!	

- Establish a follow-up communication plan with the head of the corporate HR department

For each planned action, Steve also presented a time frame for beginning and completing that step.

Now flip to Action Step 6.4 at the end of the chapter and prepare yourself for how you will communicate with your Circle.

Before turning to the next chapter, in which we're going to discuss implementing your plan and monitoring your progress, take a few minutes to read the following "Dos and Don'ts for Guides" in holding the planning meeting, to which I referred earlier.

Dos and Don'ts for Guides in Holding the Planning Meeting

No two coaching situations are identical, and it would be a mistake to expect or try to impose a uniform pattern and structure for meetings between an executive coach and a coachee or between a self-coachee and a Guide. There are, nevertheless, a number of tactical "musts" that our executive coaches always keep in mind, and that your Guide should also remember.

The following lists of *dos and don'ts* enumerate some of the most basic and universal of these. We suggest that you share them with your Guide.

Do . . .

1. Allow enough time for the meeting. If you can't create the entire plan in one meeting, schedule one or two additional sessions to complete the task.
2. Select a meeting place where you won't be interrupted and where you will have complete privacy.
3. Get the clearest possible picture of the self-coachee's situation before the meeting begins. (Have all the facts; review all the feedback.)

4. Put the self-coachee at ease.
5. Show sincere interest in the self-coachee's Intention.
6. Avoid being judgmental.
7. Consider the self-coachee's point of view as being true for him.
8. Ask open-ended questions and questions that require specific answers: Who? What? Where? When? How? How much?
9. Encourage the self-coachee to identify alternative actions.
10. Seek the self-coachee's thoughts and feelings about the possible consequences related to each alternative.
11. Avoid expressing your views too soon (i.e., telegraphing desirable responses).
12. Keep in mind that the objective is incremental change, not instant victory.

Don't . . .

1. Put the self-coachee on the defensive.
2. Be judgmental or evaluative.
3. Use the session as an opportunity to give personal advice or to sell your own ideas and values.
4. Attempt to manipulate the self-coachee's thinking.
5. Allow the session to become a psychological exercise or an emotional crisis.
6. Allow the discussion to go off on a tangent.
7. Ask leading questions.
8. Try to accomplish too much at once.
9. Ignore the fact that if lasting change is to take place, the self-coachee needs to:
    - Want to change (see the personal payoff).

- Be the final decision maker.
- "Own" the plan.

10. Rush through the session, or settle for a less-than-complete plan.

Action Step 6.1: Stories about Planning

1. What story or stories do you have about your ability to plan? Record them on www.coachyourselftowin.com or write them on a sheet of paper.
2. How did you come to create each story? What was the original event or experience in your life that brought it about? Enter this information into the table on www.coachyourselftowin.com or on paper create a table with two columns, "Story" and "Triggering Event," to help you organize your answers.

Just as you replaced the stories that were keeping you from going for your Intention, you can create replacement, or "New You," stories for those that are keeping you from developing a plan.

3. As you create "New You" stories to replace each of your old ones, ask yourself: "What story will be most helpful to me as I go about developing a plan?" Enter your answers into the template or on paper create and fill in your own table, with two columns, "Old Story" and "'New You' Story."

Action Step 6.2: Writing SMART Objectives

On www.coachyourselftowin.com or on a piece of paper, rewrite each of the following not-so-SMART objectives as a SMART objective. Use the format discussed in the chapter:

____

Action Verb (What?)

\+

____

Performance Measure (How much/How well?)

\+

____

Time Orientation (By when?)

1. NOT SO SMART: Become a financial advisor.
2. NOT SO SMART: Keep doing more and more push-ups until I reach my goal of 50.
3. NOT SO SMART: Remove junk food from my diet.
4. NOT SO SMART: Be able to speak Spanish within one month.
5. NOT SO SMART: Get a promotion.
6. NOT SO SMART: Make myself more indispensable at work.

If your answers were something like the following, you have mastered the concept of SMART objectives:

1. Pass the qualifying exams/to become a certified financial analyst/in 18 months.
2. Increase the number of push-ups I do/by 10 every week/for five weeks.
3. Eat at fast-food restaurants/no more than once a month/from now on.
4. Be able to speak enough Spanish/to go into a restaurant and order a meal/within two months.
5. Be promoted/to plant manager/within one year.
6. Take/a course in Internet marketing/within six weeks.

Action Step 6.3: Creating Your Personal Development Plan (PDP)

Sit down with your Guide and review the sample PDP for Keely J. that is included in this chapter. For additional samples, go to www.coachyourselftowin.com. Then take another look at the feedback that you received from your Circle of Support. Note the areas in which the members of your Circle agreed that you need further development and the actions that they suggested you take. Pay special attention to the watch-outs that they believe you are likely to encounter. Then complete your own PDP.

Note: You may want to create a hard-copy version as a worksheet, using the example on pages 184–185. You can then transfer your plan to the template when it is completed.

Action Step 6.4: Communicating Your Plan to Your Circle of Support

On a separate sheet of paper or on www.coachyourselftowin.com, list a few of the key actions from your PDP that you have planned to take, along with their target dates. Add this list to Step 3 of the Discussion Plan that you created in Action Step 5.1.

Self-coachee: ____________________

Overall Goal/Intention: ____________________

Guide: ____________________

Date of Plan: ____________________

Target Completion Date: ____________________

Broad and SMART Objectives	Actions	Target Date	Involvement of Others	

	Watch-Outs/ Possible Barriers to Success	Ways to Overcome Barriers	Measures/ Evidence	Status

CHAPTER 7

GETTING AND STAYING THERE

The Self-Coaching Process
1 Determine Your Self-Coachability
2 Select and Commit to an Intention
3 Identify Your Guide and Circle of Support
4 Solicit Feedback
5 Analyze and Respond to Feedback
6 Develop and Act on a Game Plan
7 Track Your Success and Recalibrate

Ten years after sailing from their homeland to wage the Trojan War, the victorious Greeks finally entered the conquered city of Troy. They celebrated and partied heartily, but they forgot one thing—to thank the gods who had fought on their side.

It turns out that this neglect wasn't very smart. When the celebrations were over, the Greeks boarded their vessels and headed for home. Little did they know that it was now payback time for the gods. The angry Olympians sent a huge storm that blew nearly all the Greek ships, including those of Odysseus, king of Ithaca, off course.

Homer's *Odyssey* goes on to recount the trials and tribulations of Odysseus and his often-foolish crew, who committed one blunder after another. Early on in their voyage, they made the mistake of enraging the sea god, Poseidon, by blinding his son, the man-eating Cyclops. Not a good idea! Poseidon vowed to avenge this act by condemning them to wander aimlessly for many years, encountering an assortment of woes, before finding their way home.

In fact, Odysseus searched for a way home for 10 more years. Each time it seemed that he was back on course, along came another obstacle—some caused by the gods, others by his men's foolishness. His clever actions—and the help of some friendly gods—almost got his entire crew home safely. But in the end, he could not control his men.

Having been warned not to stop at the Island of the Sun, Odysseus commanded his men to sail past it. When they refused, he begged them to at least not harm the cattle that lived on the island and belonged to the god of the sun. However, one day, as Odysseus slept, his men slaughtered and ate the cattle. Setting sail again, their ship was struck by a thunderbolt, and only Odysseus survived. He reached Ithaca, reclaimed his throne, and ruled the land for many years afterward.[1]

Homer's *Odyssey* isn't just one of the first action thrillers in Western literature. It is a metaphor for human life, underscoring the fact that the way to our goals is rarely a straight run. Life is full of unforeseen obstacles, and no matter how carefully we plot the course to our dreams, we are bound to run into some of them.

Which brings us full circle to Intention, and what it takes to achieve it. If we are clever, like Odysseus, we can draw on our inner resources and creativity to get around external threats. And if, like him, we are able to keep a tight rein on ourselves, we can also succeed in overcoming the barriers that we ourselves set up. If, on the other hand, we go through life acting without thinking—as Odysseus's men did—we remain our own worst enemies and have no one but ourselves to blame for our failures.

As you travel along the road to your Intention, you are bound to run into obstacles, although there is probably no Cyclops lurking in your future. Some of these difficulties will come from your environment; others will be of your own making. If you can keep on the pathway you have set for yourself and avoid giving in to despair, and if you enlist the support of your "friendly gods"—your Guide and Circle of Support—you can count on achieving the happy ending that you envisioned at the beginning of your journey.

THE NEED TO REASSESS

When we talked about developing your plan, I made the point that in executive coaching we leave as little as possible to chance. Before we begin to implement the Personal Development Plan (PDP), the executive, his supervisor, and the coach sign off on a regular coaching schedule: typically every two weeks, for two hours each time, for the duration of the coaching (usually 9 to 12 months to achieve *lasting* behavior change). The schedule—and the importance of sticking to it—is communicated to the stakeholders and anyone else in the organization who needs to be informed.

We also ensure that, when we choose a mentor and stakeholders, they will be in a position to observe the coachee's behavior on a regular basis. When they are working with the coachee on a daily or almost-daily basis, they often spot potential problems before they happen. And, of course, the coach is always scanning the environment for threats to the plan. This careful preparation is designed to eliminate as many *external* obstacles as possible. To eradicate the *internal* ones—the personal traits and self-limiting stories of the coachee—we bank on the regularity of the coaching, our skills as experienced coaches, and the fact that the stakes are generally high when an executive has been recommended for professional coaching.

Yet, even with all the preventive actions that we put in place beforehand, the executives that we coach may regress—sometimes for a brief period, occasionally permanently. Even though during the planning process you thought about possible barriers to success—the watch-outs—and ways to overcome them, by this time you know that every plan, personal or professional, is subject to the tyranny of Murphy's Law:

- The job offer you thought was definite falls through at the last minute.
- Your plan to become a real estate agent is put on hold when the housing market tanks.
- Just as you begin to see results from your diet, you receive a super-sized gift basket of the world's greatest chocolates.
- After a month off cigarettes, rumors of layoffs start flying around the office, and you're dying to light up to relieve the anxiety.
- You've finally started to build a better relationship with your teenage son when he wrecks the family car, and you lose it.
- It's becoming harder and harder to get out of bed early to go for a run, get on the treadmill, or—in my own case—do those 50 push-ups.

Barriers to reaching our Intention come in all shapes and sizes. Some are external events that we have no control over, like the downturn that causes jobs to evaporate or the beginning of Daylight Saving Time that has us getting up to exercise while it's still dark. Others are the result of changes within ourselves: after one month of dieting, we're about ready to commit murderous acts for a piece of cake, or, after having to work all day and go to school at night, we're flirting with the idea of taking up permanent residence on some tropical island. Wherever they originate, such barriers must be identified and dealt with right away so that we can get back on track.

Following is a list of the most frequent barriers that executive coachees encounter. As a self-coachee, you too may be blindsided by the same factors. If you've started out on the road to your Intention, but you aren't making the progress you'd hoped for, do a quick reassessment. Think about the traps that derail executive coachees, then ask yourself and your supporters some questions to determine whether or not they are lying in wait for you:

1. **You have no real desire to change.** Most often, stand-pattism—the belief that things are okay just as they are—is a sign of a counterfeit Intention. In executive coaching, coachees may feel compelled to go along with the coaching in order to "play the game," but deep down they believe that their behavior is fine. "Why should I change? I've gotten this far in my career without coaching."

   Ask yourself: Do I really want to do this? Hopefully, before you embarked on the self-coaching process, you read through the early chapters of this book and completed the exercises designed to test the authenticity of your Intention. But were you entirely honest with yourself? Before you go too much further, you might want to look inside yourself again, perhaps with the help of your Guide, to determine how committed you really are.

2. **The bar has been set too high; the Intention is unrealistic**. We've all seen examples of the Peter Principle at work. Sometimes people are asked to do more than they are

physically, emotionally, or intellectually capable of. No matter how hard they try, they can't morph into what's expected of them. One really sharp female executive that I coached was the heir apparent, on paper, to a very strong male CEO. She did everything she could to become a formidable leader, but it soon became apparent that the members of the senior team were never going to accept her as the next CEO. They wanted to be led by an alpha male. Our coaching helped her become an alpha female, but short of a sex-change operation, which she wasn't about to undergo, there was no way she could meet the second requirement. She moved on to a company that valued her for who she was.

Ask yourself: Did I set a realistic Intention? Once again, I would hope that you thought through the reality of your Intention and tested it with your supporters before you committed to it. But we're only human, and our reach has a way of exceeding our grasp. If you've passed out three times at the sight of blood during your first semester of medical school, you may have to rethink your Intention to become a gastroenterologist. Maybe psychiatry would be a better fit.

3. **The coachee has moved too far out of her comfort zone, too fast.** Coachees may intellectually accept the need to change. But on the emotional or psychological level, it may be just too painful. Unless the move into uncharted territory is carefully controlled and paced, the level of discomfort may become unbearable. The only way to cope is to retreat to behavior that feels natural and safe.

   Ask yourself: Am I moving too fast? Have you made so many changes or such drastic ones that you are reeling from Intention shock? If so, think seriously about reducing your speed or adding a few more pauses along the way. Get together with your Guide and rethink the time frame you've set to reach your Intention. There's more than a kernel of truth in the adages that haste makes waste and slow and steady wins the race.

4. **The coachee is under greater-than-usual stress.** I've often encountered executives who were making great progress toward becoming kinder, gentler versions of themselves: less aggressive, less authoritarian, more collaborative, and so on. Then a crisis struck. The stock value plummeted, or sales took a dive, or the competition came out with a great new product, or some new super-executive came on the scene, bringing strong competition for the next promotion. With the increased pressure, back came Rambo, guns blazing, when a team member dared disagree.

   Ask yourself: Am I going through a period of unusual stress or change? Have there been any major changes in your life, besides those that you've planned to make, since you declared your Intention? If so, the added distraction and/or stress may be diverting you from your goal. If, just when you resolved to stop smoking, a loved one was diagnosed with a life-threatening illness, the worry has no doubt intensified your desire to smoke. Or if, just as you were planning to go for that promotion to sales manager, a new hotshot joined the department, the added competition may have put you into a tailspin. It's time to reassess: Do you have to table your plan? For how long? Just a short while or indefinitely? Or can you make some modifications in the time frame, build in added supports, and come up with ways to deal with the new challenges? These questions suggest that you are at a critical crossroads. Bring your Guide and Circle of Support together and start brainstorming. The Intention they save may be your own.

5. **Old "stories" still have power, or they've been replaced with new ones that are equally limiting.** As we've seen, our stories can exercise a powerful hold on us. In the initial stages of coaching, we often devote considerable time to helping executives uncover self-limiting stories and replace them with ones that will move them forward toward their Intention. But the roots of some stories run deep, and if they aren't thoroughly debunked, they have a way of resurfacing. Or new, equally self-

limiting substitute stories pop up to replace them, requiring another round of "weeding out."

Ask yourself: Are some of my old stories still influencing my behavior, or am I sabotaging myself with new ones? Someone who has believed since kindergarten that his intelligence is lower than average is going to find it very hard to accept the fact that his mental capacity is average or above average, even when he sees the results of his IQ test. After getting some good grades, he may begin to believe that he's not so slow after all, but guess what happens the next time he fails a test? There's that negative image again, large as life, in his mind. Even when we manage to rid ourselves of our original stories, our fragile egos may devise new ones: "I realize now that I'm not really slow, but I obviously don't have the kind of intelligence that you need to get through law school."

6. **We've missed something in the environment.** Although we do our best to control the environment in which executive coaching occurs, we sometimes miss critical factors that contribute to a coachee's dysfunctional behavior. It could be a cultural mismatch or a flaw in the performance-management system that inadvertently rewards the wrong behaviors. Often, it's the relationship between the coachee and his boss, who is unknowingly contributing to the very problem he has retained us to solve. Self-coachees can also benefit from a check of their external environment: people, places, and things that may be interfering with progress toward their Intention.

   Ask yourself: Am I being held back by someone or something around me? When you put together your PDP, you may have identified people—members of your family and so-called friends—who claim to have your best interests at heart, but in fact sabotage you whenever they get the chance. Others that came to mind may have been your physical environment: a home that is too chaotic to study in or a lack of resources: not enough time, money, or support to accomplish what you need to. No matter how many potential derailers you identified, there's always the chance that you missed some. Once again, your Guide and Circle can be invaluable resources as you attempt to scan your environment for potential problems that you missed the first time around.

The sooner we become aware that a coachee has veered off course, the higher the likelihood we can get her back on the right path. The same is true in self-coaching: having an early-warning system in place will keep you from straying so far afield that you never find the way back to your Intention. That is why regular reassessment exercises, such as the one I just suggested, are a must for anyone who is in a coaching or self-coaching program.

REASSESSMENT OPTIONS

Formal Reassessments

There are two ways to conduct a reassessment: formally and informally. In the business-coaching model, we generally hold our first *formal* reassessment meeting three months after coaching begins. At this point, the coachee has received significant skills training and has had ample time to practice using the new skills on the job. Present at the meeting are the coachee, the mentor, and the coach.

I open the meeting by asking the coachee to summarize what he has been doing in the past three months to realize the Intention:

- Looking back at your Personal Development Plan, what steps have you completed?
- What results have you achieved?
- What problems have you encountered?
- How have you dealt with them?
- What have you learned?

Next, I ask for the mentor's perception:

- What actions has the coachee taken?
- What behavioral changes have you seen?
- What strengths has the coachee exhibited?
- Are there any areas of the plan in which the coachee has not made the progress that he should have by this time?
- Are you aware of anything that has impeded his progress?
- If so, is there anything you can do to eliminate that impediment?

If there's a disparity between the perceptions of the two, they need to determine why, and my role is to facilitate that conversation, then, if necessary, work with them to recalibrate the plan. I recall one case in which I was coaching an executive to become more "user-friendly": people didn't feel comfortable around him and as a result were unwilling to voice their opinions. During the meeting, the coachee ventured the opinion that he had made great progress. His mentor begged to differ: "People still aren't willing to give you feedback." As I probed for specificity, the coachee insisted, "I have made it clear that I am available any time they want to meet with me." The mentor countered with, "You are available physically, but you aren't opening up. You aren't demonstrating enough receptivity." As a result, we recalibrated his PDP, adding a new action item: gain the skills to project receptivity.

In another case, I was coaching an executive who had just been promoted and was trying to forge relationships with the members of her new team. She was doing everything I suggested, and she thought she was being accepted as "one of the gang." Her mentor, who was also her boss, commented, "I see you trying to demonstrate camaraderie, but it doesn't seem natural. It's robotic, academic—like something coming out of a book." I asked him, "How would you know when someone was demonstrating 'natural' warmth and camaraderie?" He offered a number of excellent suggestions for her to follow, and we built some skills training into her plan. The result: by the time the next reassessment came around, her mentor gave her a thumbs-up, complimenting her on the more relaxed, natural manner in which she now interacted with her team.

One note: although I don't usually go back to the stakeholders at this point, if the coachee and the mentor disagree in several areas, I may speak to a few stakeholders to validate one or the other's point of view.

At the end of the meeting, we look at the PDP once again and decide whether or not it needs to be recalibrated. If it does, we brainstorm to find the best corrective action(s), then adjust the plan accordingly. Before breaking, we schedule another reassessment meeting three months down the road. We follow this three-month schedule until the coaching ends, meeting more often only if problems arise. After the meeting, the coach prepares a Coaching Quarterly Update that is submitted to the coachee's supervisor.

Informal Reassessments

Formal reassessment meetings such as those we just described are by no means the only—or the best—way to keep track of the coachee's progress. *Informal* reassessments tend to be incident-specific in nature. Something happens to the coachee that indicates that progress is being undermined. It's time to huddle for a reassessment. Because informal reassessments are close to the "teachable moment" when an action occurs, they are often very powerful vehicles for readjusting behavior.

For example, a while back, I worked with an executive—I'll call her Janice—who had alienated many of her colleagues by "steamrolling" over them in meetings and lashing out at any who dared to disagree with her. We had three coaching sessions in which I made Janice aware of what her aggressive behavior was costing her: support for her alternatives, the ability to influence people to her point of view, the ability to advance in the company, and so on. She seemed to be showing signs of progress, but then, seven weeks into the coaching, I got an emergency call from her mentor. Several of Janice's stakeholders had proactively gone to the mentor and delivered highly negative feedback. Several times since the coaching had begun, Janice had exploded with her team. She had yelled and screamed, insulted them, and belittled their contributions.

I immediately scheduled a meeting with Janice and her mentor, who relayed the feedback from the stakeholders. At first Janice was very defensive, refusing to acknowledge the validity of her stakeholders' comments. But, as we examined the data with her, she couldn't deny the truth of the observations that had been made. She understood the need to recalibrate at this point. Together, the three of us rewrote Janice's PDP, increasing the number of coaching sessions scheduled for the next three months. It was a full-court press, designed to get her on track before further time was lost. Before long, Janice started to see the light and actually began practicing what was being preached. A few weeks later, her mentor checked in again with the stakeholders who had alerted him and was pleased when they reported seeing a real change in Janice's interactions with them.

Janice had trouble getting off the mark at the beginning. Other executives whom I've coached have come out of the gate at top speed, only to flag after a few laps. Recidivism among coachees is not uncommon—after all, we are attempting to bring about significant behavioral change, and you can't expect the habits of a lifetime to fall away in a few weeks or months. Nor is this cause for alarm—if you have a monitoring system in place. The stakeholders need to know that, no matter how far along the coaching has come, they can—and should—alert the mentor or coach if they feel that it's time to reassess.

REASSESSMENT IN SELF-COACHING

In the self-coaching arena, early and frequent reassessments (and, if indicated, recalibrations) are even more important than they are in executive coaching. In the absence of regularly scheduled coaching sessions, you are going to need to devise another way to get ongoing feedback and suggestions.

As in executive coaching, you have two options, formal and informal reassessment sessions, but it's likely that you'll opt to hold more informal meetings than our coachees do.

It's probably a good idea, however, to keep to the time schedule we use in executive coaching, at least at the beginning. Every two weeks, talk with your Guide to assess your progress and discuss any problems that you may be having. As the self-coaching proceeds, if you aren't having trouble following your plan and you are getting the results you wanted, you can always cut back on the frequency of your conversations. Not all of your interaction with your Guide has to be lengthy or formal. A quick phone call once a week to bring your Guide up to date is a good way to keep the lines of communication open.

The same is true for ongoing contact with your Circle of Support. You chose these people because you knew that they would be there for you whenever you needed them, and because you believed that they truly wanted to see you succeed. Because of this unique relationship, you will probably want to call on them more frequently than executive coachees call on their stakeholders. There are times when you'll want to sit down over lunch or dinner and talk about your progress at some length. But sometimes a quick phone call or a short e-mail is all that's needed to let a supporter know that you are still on plan.

You'll also need to stay in contact with those Circle members whose ongoing input you need in order to keep moving toward your Intention. For example, if I were going to pursue my dream of participating in a triathlon, one member of my Circle would no doubt be a nutritionist. I would meet with him at the start in order to develop a healthy regimen and perhaps set a goal of losing a certain number of pounds within the next three months. And, after the initial meeting, I would certainly check in at regular intervals to discuss any problems that I might be having with sticking to the diet and achieving the desired weight loss. If I were off plan, we might have to reduce the number of calories I was taking in or change the ratio of protein to carbohydrate.

Make sure that your supporters know that they don't have to wait for you to approach them. Remember how Steve's stakeholders took the initiative during his coaching? After they gave him their initial feedback and he explained to them his plan for becoming less U.S.-centric, he invited them to continue giving him feedback as he went through the coaching process. He asked them to let him know both when he lapsed back into his old behavior and when he succeeded in projecting a different image. They took him up on the offer, pointing out both missteps and successes and suggesting alternative ways for him to express himself.

Dealing with Relapses

The majority of people who survive heart attacks change their behavior immediately following the episode, but soon revert to their old smoking, drinking, overeating, and couch-potato ways. In fact, only 20 percent of heart attack victims permanently change their behavior.[2] The relapse rate in addiction is no less grim. Depending on the nature and severity of the addiction, anywhere from 50 to 90 percent of addicts get clean, only to go back to their drug of choice within the first year of treatment.[3]

Experts attribute this high rate of recidivism, especially in cases of recovery from life-threatening illness, to a felt reduction of risk. The proverbial "sigh of relief" reduces the sense of urgency. You drop your guard, and when you do, it's back to the same old, same old.

Once the danger is past, it is difficult, if not impossible, to recreate the initial sense of urgency that drove the person to make positive behavior changes. In my work in executive coaching, I warn coachees that the sweet smell of initial success often creates a "false positive," which then leads them to lower their guard and experience a relapse.

In discussing the issue with them, I often mention Charles Darwin's analysis of evolution. Darwin believed that species survive by adaptation. Those that can adapt to changing conditions are "fittest." They get to live another day. So, too, with anyone proceeding along the road to Intention. You must take along adaptive strategies to keep that Intention alive whenever conditions change and you drop your guard and get derailed.

I was coaching a divisional president of a large pharmaceutical company who was making steady progress toward tamping down his aggressive and controlling alpha-executive bona fides. He was feeling confident about his new leadership approach until some bad news suddenly derailed him. When his chief financial officer reported to him and his team that the quarter's numbers were way off plan, the president retreated to his old style. He went around the room and interrogated each of his subordinates in Grand Inquisitor style, ticked off a number of action items that had to be taken, and then dismissed his team members with the mandate that each of them draw up cost-cutting plans for his review within 48 hours. There was no discussion or debate. It was all about, "My will be done."

In debriefing the session with the leader, we discussed what had happened, why, what his objectives were, and how these might have been accomplished differently. Without missing a beat, he told me that he had wanted to make sure that his colleagues understood what had caused the revenue shortfall and were committed to improving the situation. I then asked him to think about his behavior in terms of these results. Did he clearly describe the situation for his team? Was time set aside to discuss possible causes? Did he elicit different points of view on alternative actions?

The leader immediately realized that his behavior might have resulted in compliance, but not commitment, and that rather than engaging his team's brainpower, he had merely succeeded in controlling it. Shortly afterward, he went into adaptive-action mode. He reconvened his team for a session in which there was frank and open discussion and debate, with everyone contributing ideas and solutions.

When you encounter a speed bump along the pathway to realizing your Intention, ask yourself, "How can I adapt to the new situation in order to ensure that I get my happy ending?" More specifically, ask yourself questions similar to the ones I posed to the executive during our debriefing: "What happened? Why? What was I trying to accomplish by derailing? How might I have behaved differently?"

Philosopher William James once said that in order to achieve peace, humans need to invent a "moral equivalent to war." James was referring to the need to find a compelling substitute that enables us to adapt to a new situation. When I first gave up cigarette smoking seven years ago, I would quit for a while, but I inevitably weakened and relapsed. It wasn't until I discovered nicotine gum that I found my "moral equivalent" to cigarettes. While it may be have been unattractive in social settings, an occasional chew, especially in situations where the temptation to light up was greatest, proved to be an effective adaptive strategy for me. It helped me to stay on Intention and off cigarettes for six years until, one year ago, I no longer needed even that support.

FEEDBACK REVISITED

Before you solicited feedback from your Guide and Circle of Support, we gave you and them some guidelines. We trust that those two sets of recommendations facilitated your initial feedback sessions with these individuals.

You will find that these guidelines are just as relevant to reassessment as they were to the initial data gathering, and it would be a good idea at this point for the members of your Circle to review the "Guidelines for Delivering Feedback." At the same time, I suggest that you go back to the "Guidelines for Receiving Feedback" to avoid the defensiveness, denial, and righteous indignation that I commonly see when coachees are told that they aren't progressing as well as they thought.

CAPTURE THE CHANGES

When you created your Personal Development Plan, you didn't carve it in stone. Hopefully, you entered the data into our template, so that you could modify it easily as you went along. As those of us who are old enough to remember manual typewriters know, computers are a godsend when it comes to updating, correcting, or editing documents. If, after reassessing, you find that you need to make changes in your plan, simply go back to the template that you downloaded and completed. I recommend that when you update the template, you enable the "track changes" feature so that your modifications are readily apparent to both you and your Guide. Even if you wrote your plan out in longhand, be sure to note alterations. Keeping changes visible keeps them top of mind.

When you make changes in the plan, should you inform your Circle of Support? In executive coaching, we don't usually go back to the stakeholders with a revised plan. In fact, we don't usually share the entire plan with them at all. As you'll recall from our discussion of Steve's postplanning conversation with his stakeholders, he gave them a top-line summary of what he was planning to do, without going into great detail and without giving them a copy of his PDP. This is appropriate in business coaching, where most of the planned actions involve only the executive and her mentor and coach. Of course, any stakeholders who are going to play a major role in the intervention need to be kept abreast of changes.

In self-coaching, there are some good reasons for sharing the entire plan with your Circle and keeping its members informed of any changes you make in it. First, you asked these people to support you because you valued their opinion, and the feedback that they provided to you probably included a number of suggested actions and watch-outs. Showing them that you have incorporated these into your plan is a way of thanking them and keeping them motivated to provide ongoing feedback.

Second, in the absence of a professional coach, some members of your Circle may have volunteered to help you achieve a specific portion of the plan. If the amount of time you are going to need from them or the nature of their involvement changes, you need to let them know.

Remember, apart from some professionals for whose services you may be paying, your supporters are doing this out of a desire to see you succeed. Keep them in the loop; it's a courtesy that they deserve.

RETHINKING YOUR INTENTION

Reassessment is a powerful tool for getting you back on the path to your Intention after you've strayed. It's also a way to find out whether or not you are actually on the right road. The female executive I spoke about earlier, who no matter how hard she tried was never going to be an acceptable successor to her alpha-male predecessor, is a case in point. Her Intention wasn't counterfeit; she did everything right as she tried to remake herself in his image. Through no fault of her own, it just wasn't enough, and she finally realized that she would be better off trading her original Intention for one that was "doable": finding a CEO position in a company that wasn't averse to female leaders.

There are many reasons why a coachee may decide to abandon an Intention and perhaps replace it with another. My wife and I know a woman who was determined to make her marriage work. Bev and her husband fought about everything: how to discipline the children, how to spend their money, how to decorate the house, where to celebrate holidays, where to go on vacation, and on and on. Year after year, she hung in there, trying to resolve their differences. They went to a marriage counselor, at her insistence. They took a second honeymoon to "rekindle the flame." She cooked his favorite meals, watched football games with him, and encouraged him to go out with the guys. It was her Intention to stay married, no matter what the cost to her own happiness and self-esteem.

After a long heart-to-heart with another friend, who pointed out all the things that Bev had done to keep the marriage together and the fact that her efforts had been futile, it finally struck Bev that she should replace her undoable Intention with another: end the marriage with as little pain as possible to her, her husband, and her children.

Was Bev a failure because she didn't achieve her original Intention? I don't believe so. In life as in poker, you need to know when to hold 'em and when to fold 'em. If you can honestly say that you have done your best, but you still can't achieve your Intention, then it's probably time to move on. Don't do so without consulting your Guide and your Circle of Support, however. As objective observers, they may have a clearer view of your true situation, and may be able to get you over something that is merely a speed bump. Or, if you are in fact right about the unreachability of your Intention, they can validate your conclusion and perhaps suggest a more achievable goal.

RULES OF THE ROAD TO YOUR INTENTION

Reality is unpredictable. I've never seen a plan go from Intention to actuality in a single leap. As you work toward your Intention in real time, these seven rules of the road should help to keep you on your path:

1. **Expect the unexpected**. Wouldn't it be nice if life hung in suspended animation, waiting for your plan to fully materialize? Don't count on it. "Life is what happens to you while you're busy making other plans." John Lennon was right. Don't expect a straight path from plan to Intention. That's unrealistic, and such an expectation can have a chilling effect on your will to succeed. The unexpected is a fact of life, not a sign of weakness or error.

2. **Focus on the controllable**. Consider how one Olympic gold medalist, American Nordic combined skier Todd Lodwick, prepares for the rigors of international competition. "I've learned to focus on what I can control, like my training, my equipment,

my race strategy, and be aware of what I can't control, like the weather, the quality of the snow, or my competitors. I use the image of a brick on a balance—I want the 'bricks' from the things I can control to outweigh the 'bricks' on the other side of the scale."[4] Your "bricks" are the steps in your plan, and they should outweigh what you can't control. Remember, your plan is your creation. While the unexpected lurks, you are in control, and you can make adjustments if required.

3. **Develop a routine**. "A foolish consistency is the hobgoblin of little minds," according to American philosopher Ralph Waldo Emerson. Maybe so, but when consistency forms itself into a routine, it serves as an effective helpmate to your Intention. When the behaviors required to implement your plan become part of your built-in repertoire, you move toward your Intention with little resistance. No need to worry about the hobgoblin of consistency; inconsistency is the real villain that takes you off plan.

4. **Hold fast**. The Bible enjoins us, "But examine everything carefully; hold fast that which is good."[5] This is sound advice that will serve you well as you implement your plan. If your plan is not getting you to your Intention, examine the situation carefully and be prepared to make a midcourse correction or change. But if you're moving steadily ahead, hold fast to the course you have set. Or, in today's language: if it ain't broke, don't fix it.

5. **Fail smart**. If you stray from the pathway that takes you to your Intention, get up, dust yourself off, and begin anew. But learn. Why waste failure? As Henry Ford put it, "Failure is only the opportunity to begin again, only this time more wisely."

   And realize that perfection is an ideal, and that setbacks are not a catastrophe. Recently, CNN.com carried a story about a woman who has lost 70 pounds and kept the weight off. She commented, "Every choice I make is an on-plan choice. If I choose to eat a doughnut, that's fine. I'm going to eat that doughnut. It doesn't mean I'm off my diet. I'll account for that in a later meal. Or I'll have a lighter dinner." What this lady is practicing might be called the law of compensation: sure, you can "cheat," provided you compensate immediately so that you stay on plan.

6. **Think creatively**. If you feel that you are in a rut, or your progress is too slow, or you are beginning to waver in your Intention, it's time to expand your options. Here, it's important not to swing wildly at different alternatives, hoping that you'll land some knockout punch that will bring victory. "Never confuse motion with action," said Benjamin Franklin. If you do, you're likely to get stuck in an activity trap. Go back to your Intention and the objectives that you set in your Personal Development Plan: Do they suggest alternative ways of acting? Review your inputs to the self-coaching process: Do they open up options? Are there stories you are holding on to that need reframing? Do your Guide and the members of your Circle of Support have suggestions? Look at our section entitled "Additional Resources for Self-Coachees" for suggested reading and Web sites. Get going, not stuck!
7. **Pack a parachute**. As you proceed along the pathway to your Intention, remember to build in contingencies. This way, not only will you expect the unexpected, but you'll be prepared to act. Keep your eye on the watch-outs in your plan: "What if?" These are two very powerful words to ask during the implementation phase. And then: "If so, what will I do?" To land safely, the best parachute is a good plan.

ARRIVAL

Ah, the sweet smell of success! As you near the end of your journey to your Intention, it's in the air around you. But how can you be sure that the heady fragrance is the real thing and not a sensory hallucination?

In many cases, there's no doubt about it: you have clear, measurable proof that you've reached your goal. You look at the scale and see that you've dropped the 20 pounds you were so determined to lose; you pick up your college diploma from the frame shop and hang it on the wall for all to see; you compare your old pay stub to the one you're receiving now that you've been made supervisor. You have hard, positive proof that you have turned your Intention into reality.

But what if the Intention you chose to pursue was less tangible? Maybe you wanted to improve your relationship with your family. How would you know that you had achieved your Intention? Likewise for a self-coachee whose goal was to be perceived as a stronger leader. How would she assess the degree to which she had succeeded?

The answers can be found in the first chapter of this book, where I mentioned that I learned early in my executive coaching that my primary concern was about *changing observable behavior*. In my view, this is the only reliable indicator of performance and the only way to measure the success of a coachee or self-coachee.

As we've gone through the self-coaching process together, you too have focused on changing your observable behavior. You began by asking your Guide and your Circle of Support to describe your past behavior and how it might affect your ability to achieve your Intention. You also asked them to suggest alternative behaviors that would advance you toward your Intention. As you adopted these new behaviors, you went back to your supporters periodically to ask them how well you were doing.

Now, as you approach the target date that you set for the realization of your Intention, it's time to ask those supporters one last time, "Is my behavior aligned with my Intention? Have I taken my game up to a new level? Do you see a new me?"

The Last Word on Steve

In executive coaching, one final reassessment is conducted about a month before the projected closeout date, either by the mentor or by the coach. In the case of my coachee, Steve, we had contracted for a year of coaching, so at the 11-month mark, Steve's mentor went back to the stakeholders and asked how Steve's behavior had changed since we first gathered feedback from them.

As you'll recall, Steve's behavior change encompassed five objectives, everything from strengthening his leadership presence to building his team.

Here's the new book on Steve, as reported by his stakeholders:

- He acts more confidently than he used to.
- He is taking more risks—putting his points of view out there.
- He isn't as introverted.
- He has become a better listener and isn't so defensive.
- He met with each of us individually and asked for our ideas, feelings, and concerns about having a new team leader.
- There's a relaxed feeling in team meetings now.
- He no longer uses Americanisms.
- He isn't as aloof from us as he was at the beginning; he's really starting to connect.

Steve and his organization have "gotten there."

YOUR JOURNEY ENDS—AND CONTINUES

Intentions come in a number of varieties. Goal-specific Intentions, such as seeking a new career or running a marathon, represent defined accomplishments with a clear beginning, middle, and end to the journey.

Other Intentions are equally goal-specific, but once the goal is achieved, there is a continuing need to reassess and recalibrate, lest you fall back on old behaviors. Redefining workplace behavior, changing family relationships, and eliminating bad habits all fall into this category. Here, Intention is not a one-off event, a graduation day on which you complete some prescribed curriculum and move on. It is more dynamic. You must remain *in* your Intention, always conscious of the progress you've made and alert to potential breakdowns.

At this moment, feel great pride that you have "gotten there." You deserve to celebrate. You have held fast to your Intention, and *you* wrote the script. And, best of all, it's not a movie. It's the New You.

So, gather together your Guide and Circle of Support and thank them for all they've done to bring about your achievement. Tell them how much you appreciate the role they played in your success. Raise your glasses in a toast to one another, to an Intention realized, to other journeys that you will surely be taking, and to other Intentions that self-coaching will enable you to achieve.

The Self-Coaching Process
1 Determine Your Self-Coachability
2 Select and Commit to an Intention
3 Identify Your Guide and Circle of Support
4 Solicit Feedback
5 Analyze and Respond to Feedback
6 Develop and Act on a Game Plan
7 Track Your Success and Recalibrate

NOTES

Introduction

1. Caryn Rousseau, "Oprah 'Mad, Embarrassed' about Weight Gain," *accessAtlanta,* December 9, 2008; www.accessatlanta.com.
2. Oprah Winfrey, "How Did I Let This Happen Again?" *O, The Oprah Magazine*, January 2009; http://www.oprah.com/article/health/200901_ omag_oprah_weight/28.
3. American Lung Association, "Freedom from Smoking"; http://www.lungusa.org/assets/documents/program-pdfs/freedom-from-smoking.pdf.
4. American Heart Association, "Statistics You Need to Know"; http://www.americanheart.org/presenter.jhtml?identifier = 107.
5. Jennifer B. McClure, Group Health Center for Health Studies; http://www.grouphealthresearch.org/research/areas/behavior.aspx.
6. Albert Ellis and Robert A. Harper, *A Guide to Rational Living*, 3rd ed. (Hollywood, Calif.: Melvin Powers Wilshire Book Company, 1997), p. 6.
7. Jared Fogle with Anthony Bruno, *Jared, the Subway Guy* (New York: St. Martin's Press, 2006).
8. Carlo DiClemente and James O. Prochaska, "The Transtheoretical Model of Behavior Change," The HABITS Lab at UMBC; http://www.umbc.edu/psyc/habits/content/the_model/index.html.
9. If you have ever been through erhard seminars training, or *est*, as it's better known, you know that for many it was a gut-wrenching, life-changing experience. At the end of the first

weekend, people were often shattered and weeping uncontrollably because they had faced, for the first time, long-buried truths about themselves. Which is why, before people signed up for the program, est organizers always asked them if their life was currently in a breakdown. If the answer was yes, they were advised not to enroll until their life was back under control. Although self-coaching is nowhere near as traumatic, looking into the mirror for the first time can be a challenging experience.

Chapter 1

1. Eckhart Tolle, *The Power of Now* (Novato, Calif.: New World Library and Vancouver, B.C., Canada: Namaste Publishing, 2004), pp. 119–120.
2. Melinda Beck, "Silencing the Voice That Says You're a Fraud," *Wall Street Journal*, June 16, 2009.
3. Albert Ellis and Robert A. Harper, *A Guide to Rational Living*, 3rd ed. (Hollywood, Calif.: Melvin Powers Wilshire Book Company, 1997), p. 3.
4. Albert Ellis has a number of therapeutic techniques to help people resolve issues of self-worth and overgeneralization. One of these, "Teaching Clients Unconditional Self-Acceptance (USA)," is explained in *Overcoming Destructive Beliefs, Feelings, and Behaviors* (Amherst, N.Y.: Prometheus Books, 2001), pp. 24–28.
5. Carlo DiClemente and James O. Prochaska, "The Transtheoretical Model of Behavior Change," The HABITS Lab at UMBC; http://www.umbc.edu/psyc/habits/content/the_model/index.html.
6. Ellis and Harper, *Rational Living*, p. 26.

Chapter 2

1. Joseph L. Wions, *From Nightmares to Miracles: A Quest for Recovery from ALS*, unpublished manuscript.

2. Aristotle, *Nicomachean Ethics*, trans. Hippocrates G. Apostle (Grinnell, Iowa: Peripatetic Press, 1975), p. 42.
3. Grade Saver, "Aristotle's Ethics Study Guide"; http://www.gradesaver.com/aristotles-ethics/study-guide/section3/.
4. Wayne W. Dyer, *The Power of Intention* (Carlsbad, Calif.: Hay House, Inc., 2004), p. 4.
5. Ibid., pp. 16–17.
6. Werner Erhard discussed his concept of "context" with Tom Snyder on January 31, 2009. To view the video, visit http://www.youtube.com/watch?v = psxsVh90Rbw.
7. Albert Ellis and Robert A. Harper, *A Guide to Rational Living*, 3rd ed. (Hollywood, Calif.: Melvin Powers Wilshire Book Company, 1997), p. xii.
8. Ibid., p. 31.
9. Oprah Winfrey, "How Did I Let This Happen Again?" *O, The Oprah Magazine*, January 2009; http://www.oprah.com/article/health/200901_ omag_oprah_weight/28.
10. Ibid.
11. Dyer, *Power of Intention*, p. 87.
12. Wions, *From Nightmares to Miracles*.
13. Ibid.

Chapter 3

1. SCORE Success Stories; http://www.score.org/success_jelly_belly.html.
2. Ibid.
3. Charles Horton Cooley, *Human Nature and the Social Order* (New York: Scribner's, 1902), pp. 179–185.
4. Michel de Montaigne; http://www.inspirational-quotes.info/thoughts.html.
5. http://selfimprovementbase.com/618/the-value-of-a-mentor.
6. Lindsay Dunlap, "One Size Does Not Fit All," December 11, 2008; http://www.neversaydiet.com/blog-article/surprise-oprahs-normal.

7. Matthew 7:7, *The Holy Bible Containing the Old and New Testaments*, Authorized King James Version (Westport, Conn.: Trinity Publishing Company). (The same advice is given in Luke 11:9.)
8. Malia Wollan, "The Big Draw of a GPS Run," *New York Times*, Blogging Times article, August 20, 2009; http://www.nytimes.com/2009/08/20/fashion/20GPS.html?_r=1,
9. SCORE Success Stories; http://www.score.org/success_vera_bradley.html.

Chapter 4

1. Adapted from Kevin Eikenberry, "Balancing Positive and Negative Feedback"; http://www.hodu.com/balance-feed.shtml.
2. Karen Knee, "Psychology of Thriving," July 6, 2009; www.philly.com, p. 3.

Chapter 5

1. Theodor Reik, *Listening with the Third Ear* (New York: Farrar, Straus and Co., 1948), pp. 174–175.
2. Douglas Wolk, "Never Broadcast Your Relationship Status," *Wired*, Issue 17.08, July 15, 2009; http://www.wired.com/culture/lifestyle/magazine/17-08/by_broadcast_relationship.

Chapter 6

1. Aesop, "The Ant and the Grasshopper"; http://www.dltk-teach.com/fables/grasshopper/mstory.html.
2. Quoted in Robert I. Sutton, "Beware the Cone of Silence," *Harvard Business Review*, June 2009, p. 48.
3. Cited in "A Dull, Heavy Calm," *The Economist*, October 1, 2009, p. 26.
4. Adapted from Arina Nikitina, "SMART Goal Setting: A Surefire Way to Achieve Your Goals," *Goal Setting Guide*; http://www.goal-setting-guide.com/smart-goals.html.

Chapter 7

1. Homer, *The Odyssey*, trans. E. V. Rieu (Baltimore, Md.: Penguin Books, 1962).
2. Ronald Heifets, Alexander Grashow, and Marty Linsky, "Leadership in a (Permanent) Crisis," *Harvard Business Review,* July–August 2009, p. 64.
3. F. Curtis Breslin, Martin Zack, and Shelley McMain, "An Information-Processing Analysis of Mindfulness: Implications for Relapse Prevention in the Treatment of Substance Abuse," *Clinical Psychology: Science and Practice* 9, no. 3 (Fall 2002), p. 275.
4. James M. Citrin, "Performance Lessons from Olympians," *Wall Street Journal online*, October 2, 2009.
5. 1 Thessalonians 5:21, *New American Standard Bible,* online edition; http://fliiby.com/file/64978/4badsrsrfh.html.

ADDITIONAL RESOURCES FOR SELF-COACHEES

Additional Resources provides a select number of publications, Web sites, and organizations for readers seeking to deepen their knowledge of various self-help related areas, ranging from addiction to coaching to personal change, health, relationships, and careers. It is meant to be a suggestive, "get me started" list.

ADDICTION

National Clearinghouse for Alcohol and Drug Information, U.S. Department of Health and Human Services, Substance Abuse and Mental Health Services Administration

http://ncadi.samhsa.gov

The U.S. Department of Health and Human Services sponsors this massive Web site under the auspices of the Substance Abuse and Mental Health Services Administration. Its navigation tools enable you to search by drug (including alcohol and nicotine), audience (from "Rural Communities" to "Children of Abusers"), or issue ("Binge Drinking," "Juvenile Justice," and several dozen more).

Though the site is complicated, and you'll find yourself linking to separate but related government sources, take the time to browse. Especially impressive are the lengthy lists of publications that are available at no cost and the Treatment Facility Locator (under "Resources"). For the research-minded, the statistics and reports that are available are almost overwhelmingly plentiful.

Twelve-Step "Anonymous" Programs

The twelve-step program that lies at the heart of Alcoholics Anonymous has been adapted by an array of organizations that support members in stopping and recovering from negative behaviors. Some of these sites are more complete than others, but all of them offer an outline of the program and ways to find a support group in your area. (Many of them also have links to additional resources, newsletters, conferences, and other such material.)

Cocaine Anonymous
 www.ca.org/
Clutterers Anonymous
 http://sites.google.com/site/clutterersanonymous/Home
Debtors Anonymous
 www.debtorsanonymous.org/
Food Addicts Anonymous
 www.foodaddictsanonymous.org/
Gamblers Anonymous
 www.gamblersanonymous.org/
Marijuana Anonymous
 www.marijuana-anonymous.org/
Overeaters Anonymous
 www.oa.org/
Nicotine/Smokers Anonymous
 www.nicotine-anonymous.org/
Workaholics Anonymous
 www.workaholics-anonymous.org/

ADDICTION—ALCOHOL

Alcoholics Anonymous

www.aa.org

Its mission is clear and is known worldwide: "Alcoholics Anonymous is a fellowship of men and women who share with one another their experience, strength, and hope that they may solve their common problem and help others to recover from alcoholism.

The only requirement for membership is a desire to stop drinking." AA's phenomenal success rate speaks for itself.

The very sophisticated AA Web site is packed with brochures, videos, links, and background information for every audience: professionals, members of the media, public officials, and, of course, those seeking recovery.

ADDICTION—FOOD

Michelle May, *Eat What You Love, Love What You Eat: How to Break Your Eat-Repent-Repeat Cycle* (Austin, Tex.: Greenleaf Book Group Press, 2009)

Dr. Michelle May is a practicing family physician and, by her own admission, a reformed yo-yo dieter. Her first book, *Am I Hungry? What to Do When Diets Don't Work*, introduced the premise of replacing repeated dieting attempts with a long-term, healthy relationship with food. That concept has come to full fruition in *Eat What You Love*.

The opening section, entitled "Think," outlines the basic questions in the Eating Cycle that govern our relationship with food. In what Dr. May calls instinctive eating, the questions and answers are straightforward. The answer to "When do I eat?" is simple: when I'm hungry. "How much do I eat?": enough to satisfy my hunger. When our relationship with food is unbalanced, the answer to the "when" question reflects that imbalance: "when I'm upset" or "when I need a break from my stressful schedule," for example. When we introduce a restrictive model—through a specific diet plan, for example—the answers may be just as out of balance: what I eat is based on external rules, rather than my own desires. In short, we have lost the equilibrium that promotes a healthy, self-regulating relationship with food.

May's remaining chapters include "Nourish," with information about nutritional values and food choices; "Live," on the activity that we include in our daily routines; and, "Eat," a collection of healthy recipes from May's professional chef husband. Taken as a whole, these insights into why we eat (or don't), exercise (to earn the right to eat?), and live the way we do support a return to eating—and living—"fearlessly and mindfully."

This is a very understandable and sensible work, already acclaimed by other physicians and based on sound science.

National Eating Disorders Association

www.nationaleatingdisorders.org

Eating disorders affect people of all genders, races, nationalities, and socioeconomic statuses. The best known, anorexia nervosa, is associated with the highest mortality rate among mental illnesses. If you suspect that you or a loved one has an eating disorder, seek professional help. The principles of self-coaching may eventually be useful, but the underlying mental illness must first be addressed.

The Web site of the National Eating Disorders Association (NEDA) is an outstanding and immediately available resource. Look no further. Visit the site for downloadable toolkits for parents and educators, stories of recovery, and links to resources of every kind imaginable. NEDA's mission is "to support those affected by eating disorders and be a catalyst for prevention, cures, and access to quality care."

Weight Watchers International

www.weightwatchers.com

The Weight Watchers approach to weight loss was conceived more than 40 years ago in small weekly meetings of friends at the home of founder Jean Nidetch. Those small gatherings have grown into an enormous commercial entity providing weight management methods, support, and products. But it's hard to argue with success; this enduring and sensible approach to weight control has helped millions of people around the world.

A variety of tools now offer alternatives to the well-known weekly meetings associated with Weight Watchers. Weight Watchers Online enables subscribers to track their daily intake and progress against goals and provides access to support for an overall healthy lifestyle, including recipes, workout programs, and tips on keeping eating under control during the workday. Check out Weight Watchers

Mobile, a cell phone application that interacts with the online service to calculate and track your daily "points" in real time.

David Zinczenko and Matt Goulding, *Eat This, Not That 2010! The No-Diet Weight Loss Solution* (Emmaus, Pa.: Rodale, 2010)

This latest entry in the *Eat This, Not That!* series matches its predecessors for useful information, browsability—and lots of surprises. The authors compare similar foods—a taco and a burrito from Taco Bell, for example—and bust myth after myth about making food choices.

Eating out, scanning the grocery shelves, negotiating with the kids: no matter what the situation, these *Men's Health* editors point out the pitfalls. They focus on the benefits of choosing foods that are higher in protein and fiber and lower in fats, sugar, and sodium. Cutesy but painful reminders of the exercise you'd need to do to expend the calories in a less-healthful choice are sprinkled throughout.

An intentionally lightweight but helpful guide to choosing wisely while on the go.

ADDICTION—GAMBLING

National Council on Problem Gambling

http://www.ncpgambling.org

The National Council on Problem Gambling was created in 1972 with two founding principles: advocacy for problem gamblers and their families, and a refusal to take a political position on legalized gambling. That clarity and objectivity are demonstrated on its Web site, which offers a rich array of resources for problem gamblers, counseling professionals, state and local affiliates, and the public.

Especially helpful are the tools for problem gamblers that are immediately accessible on the site: pathological gambling criteria, a counselor search, "Help by State," links to self-help organizations (Gamblers Anonymous, for example), and an online workbook.

NCPG operates a national help line, certifies professionals in gambling counseling, holds an annual conference on problem gambling, and sponsors National Problem Gambling Awareness Week (see www.npgaw.org).

ADDICTION—SPENDING

Debtors Anonymous

http://www.debtorsanonymous.org

An addiction to compulsive spending can quickly pull addicts and their loved ones into a life-destroying pattern of debt. Debtors Anonymous (DA) is "a fellowship of men and women who share their experience, strength and hope with each other so that they may solve their common problem and help others to recover from compulsive debting."

This site provides access to accurate information, self-assessment tools, and links to local DA chapters, where sufferers can find a network of support for recovery. Online and telephone meetings are also available. For more information, order the organization's book of recovery stories, *A Currency of Hope*, online.

ADDICTION—TOBACCO

American Lung Association

http://www.lungusa.org/stop-smoking

The American Lung Association does a fine job of advocating nationally for tobacco control and providing information about smoking and its effects (a Spanish translation is also available). But the real value here is in the information and support for those who are ready to quit. A bonus: look for the link to *Helping Smokers Quit: State Cessation Coverage*. It's a report on the status of health insurance coverage of quit-smoking programs.

Check out the direct link to the ALA's no-cost, personalized Freedom from Smoking Online program at http://www.ffsonline.org/.

Allen Carr, *The Easy Way to Stop Smoking: Join the Millions Who Have Become Non-Smokers Using Allen Carr's EasyWay Method* (New York: Sterling, 2010)

Carr first developed his principles for stopping addictive behaviors when he gave up his own five-pack-a-day habit in 1983. He captured what worked for him in the first edition of this book, and since then, he has written companion volumes on controlling alcohol use, achieving weight loss, and even attaining success and managing worries—all with his EasyWay method.

The success of Carr's method speaks for itself. A network of 70 EasyWay clinics operates in major cities in 30 countries. Actor Anthony Hopkins endorses the method on Carr's Web site (www.allencarr.com). So what's the secret?

Carr promises (and apparently delivers) "instantaneous" freedom from the addiction that has driven your life and endangered your health. He is clear that relying on personal willpower is ineffective. Instead, Carr addresses the reasons that we acquire and continue the addiction. For smokers, for example, he explodes the myth that "smoking relieves stress," explains the science of nicotine addiction, and gives detailed advice on handling withdrawal symptoms. His approach to controlling alcohol consumption is decidedly different from that of Alcoholics Anonymous; he does not advise the reader to surrender her will to a higher power, but instead portrays the use of alcohol as physically and emotionally devastating.

The arguments that Carr presents are intellectually reasoned, but also powerfully motivating. In each work, Carr encourages you to continue drinking, smoking, whatever, until you have finished the book and you can fully—and joyfully!—embrace your newfound freedom with a final toast. An utterly down-to-earth, readable approach, with intriguing results.

Tobacco Control Research Branch of the National Cancer Institute

http://www.smokefree.gov

Try this practical, straightforward site for the basics of quitting smoking. Links to other government sites are provided, but stick to the main menu to get down-to-earth information and strategies for quitting. Free resources include an online "quit guide" (also available in print); online self-assessment tools on depression, stress, and withdrawal; and information for contacting a smoking counselor via instant messaging or telephone. All topics are clearly presented and easy to digest.

Smokefree.gov was created by the Tobacco Control Research Branch of the National Cancer Institute.

COACHING—EXECUTIVE

Marshall Goldsmith, *What Got You Here Won't Get You There: How Successful People Become Even More Successful* (New York: Hyperion, 2007)

Marshall Goldsmith is a guru in the field of executive coaching. He's been named one of the top 10 executive educators by the *Wall Street Journal*, and the American Management Association has selected him as one of its "50 greatest thinkers."

This volume is dedicated to already-successful leaders who "want to take it to the next level"; however, any self-coach could draw valuable personal lessons from Goldsmith's list of "20 Workplace Habits You Need to Break." Those habits will ring true for most of us: telling the world how smart we are, not listening, and making excuses, for example. In straightforward language and examples, Goldsmith explains the negative consequences of these and other habits of our thinking.

Take a look at the many resources available from this lauded coach on www.marshallgoldsmithlibrary.com. And look for his book, *Mojo: How to Get It, How to Keep It, and How to Get It Back If You Lose It.*

International Coach Federation

http://www.coachfederation.org

For more information on the profession of coaching; training, and credentialing for coaches; and finding a professional coach, look to the International Coach Federation (ICF), a nonprofit membership association. Follow the "Find a Coach" link to access the ICF Coach Referral Service or Member Directory and read tips on choosing a coach of your own.

Laura Whitworth and Karen Kimsey-House, Henry Kimsey-House, and Phillip Sandahl, *Co-Active Coaching: New Skills for Coaching People Toward Success in Work and Life*, 2nd ed. (Mountain View, Calif.: Davies-Black Publishing, 2007)

With her early practice and broad experience, Whitworth helped to usher in the age of professional coaching. She and her colleagues created a model of co-active coaching on the premise that any coaching must be driven by the client's agenda—and, although they may not realize it, most clients already know or can find the answers that they are seeking.

Two additional cornerstones support the co-active model: co-active coaching addresses the client's whole life, and the coaching relationship is a designed alliance. The skills and practices identified by the authors as central to coaching—intuition, listening, and curiosity—are attributes that will inform any process of self-examination as well.

The book is filled with coaching dialogues and examples, skill-building exercises, and an extended toolkit of worksheets, exercises, and forms to use with clients. This second edition also includes a CD. Self-coachees will find these tools useful for their own work and can rest assured that the experts agree that the answers are already within their grasp.

COACHING—SELF

H. A. Dorfman, *Coaching the Mental Game: Leadership Philosophies and Strategies for Peak Performance in Sports—and Everyday Life* (Lanham, Md.: Taylor Trade Publishing, 2003)

From the Foreword: "Coaching is teaching in its most perfect and rewarding form. No matter what the sport, coaches are basically giving information, waiting for a response, and then giving feedback on that response."

If the athletic model of coaching and leadership resonates with your plans for self-coaching, check out this dense but absorbing book. Dorfman shares his methods for coaching the mental aspects of any sport—or any life undertaking. Major sections are devoted to leadership style and substance, communication processes and techniques, and impact terms from the perspective of both coach and athlete.

Thomas J. Leonard with Byron Laursen, *The Portable Coach: 28 Surefire Strategies for Business and Personal Success* (New York: Scribner, 1998)

A one-time financial planner who found his clients asking for all kinds of advice ("What color Mercedes should we buy?"), Leonard has been called the "patriarch" of personal coaching. In 1992, he founded Coach U(niversity), and its programs and workshops for aspiring practitioners helped to codify coaching as a profession. From this first dot-com project, Leonard went on to create teleclasses for coaching and other online ventures; he founded the International Coach Federation in 1994.

In this book, Leonard devotes a chapter to each of his "28 Principles of Attraction": principles that are intended to help you consistently attract opportunities, rewarding relationships, strong finances, and so on. The flexibility of this book lies in the standalone value of each of the chapters. Leonard deliberately invites you to start anywhere and let your interests lead the way. Each self-contained topic includes an overview of the principle, six to ten practical ways to implement it, self-assessment tests, and how to evaluate your progress in each area. Among the 28 are "Become Incredibly Selfish," "Eliminate Delay," and "Develop More Character than You Need."

Other related resources:

- *The 28 Laws of Attraction: Stop Chasing Success and Let It Chase You* (Leonard's second book)
- *Coach Yourself to Success: 101 Tips from a Personal Coach for Reaching Your Goals at Work and in Life*, by Talane Miedaner (Lincolnwood, Ill.: Contemporary Books, 2000). An enjoyable,

browsable book from a successful life coach, in the tradition of Coach University and Thomas Leonard.

Joseph J. Luciani, *The Power of Self-Coaching: The Five Essential Steps to Creating the Life You Want* (Hoboken, N.J.: Wiley, 2004)

Over the course of a 25-year practice in psychology, Luciani has concluded that personal change is indeed possible. As a clinical therapist, he emphasizes the need to take responsibility for choosing to change rather than suffering the chronic unhappiness that we've grown used to.

Luciani's earlier work, *Self Coaching,* focused on addressing issues of anxiety and depression. This book is a broader exploration of Luciani's self-coaching technique, developed through the courageous work of his clients. The book includes many self-quizzes, exercises, and self-coaching "Power Drills" to help readers recognize and move beyond negative habits. The five principles of Self Talk that constitute the third section of the book are the underpinnings of his process approach to coaching.

See the Web site http://www.self-coaching.net.

Germaine Porche and Jed Niederer, *Coach Anyone about Anything: How to Help People Succeed in Business and Life* (Del Mar, Calif.: Wharton Publishing, 2001)

Although this guide was written as a short reference for professional coaches, a number of its tools and concepts will be useful for those who are self-coaching.

The authors have trained thousands of coaches under the auspices of the CoachLab Division of Eagle's View Systems (see www.eaglesview.com). This handbook is chock-full of short lists of questions and exercises, as well as figures that illustrate key coaching concepts: the difference between Actions and Activity; the coaching spectrum from Content to Process expertise; and how

"Weight," "Drag," "Thrust," and "Lift" factors affect your ability to achieve a stated outcome.

This book may be most helpful to those who have agreed to serve as your Guide or as members of your Circle of Support during your self-coaching experience; the sections on listening and advice are insightful. For yourself, be sure to read the examples of Coaching Outcomes Contracts; these are solid models for you to consider while setting your own goals.

GENERAL

David Allen, *Making It All Work: Winning at the Game of Work and the Business of Life* (New York: Penguin, 2008)

David Allen's first book, *Getting Things Done*, triggered an enormous response around the globe from those who were looking for a method of "personal organizing" that would help busy people ease their stress while juggling complex priorities. (That means *all* of us!) The "GTD" phenomenon spawned hundreds of active blogs and rapid adoption, particularly in high-tech companies, where adherents quickly converted Allen's "lists" and "buckets" technique for use with their existing organizing software (like Microsoft Outlook).

This follow-up volume reviews the basics of GTD for readers and provides details of the method in its extensive appendixes. The core chapters are devoted to the two concepts that drive GTD: gaining control over the to-dos of all kinds that race through our heads, and gaining perspective on how competing priorities and tasks measure up. If you're a list maker by nature—and especially if you're not—you're sure to make your day more productive, even if you adopt only one or two of Allen's tips and methods.

Also by David Allen: *Ready for Anything: 52 Productivity Principles for Work and Life.*

Adelaide Bry, *est (erhard seminars training): 60 Hours That Transform Your Life* (New York: Avon Books, 1976)

This psychology-trained author's account of the principles and practices of est recalls the 1970s cultural phenomenon founded by Zen-influenced Werner Erhard. Erhard described his legendary 60-hour sessions as "designed to transform the level at which you experience life so that living becomes a process of expanding satisfaction." Through word of mouth from participants, thousands came to appreciate its lessons of abandoning tired beliefs and attending to immediate experience.

Stephen R. Covey, *The 7 Habits of Highly Effective People: Powerful Lessons in Personal Change* (New York: Free Press, 1989; London: Simon & Schuster, 2004)

Any businessperson who's been offered a book on personal development in the last 20 years has probably heard of this one. It's wildly popular with individuals and prominently displayed in managers' offices around the world.

Covey's landmark work is described as "a holistic, integrated, principle-centered approach for solving personal and professional problems." Habits, he argues, are created (or broken) on the basis of knowledge, skills, and desire; all three elements are required. His central thesis is that each of us must first establish personal independence (Habits 1 through 3, which constitute our Private Victory), then grow into the mature paradigm of interdependence (our Public Victory, Habits 4 through 6). The seventh habit is a basic: ongoing physical, mental, spiritual, and emotional renewal to support our commitment to the other six.

In the afterword to the 2004 edition, Covey notes, "You can pretty well sum up the first three habits with the expression 'make and keep a promise.' And . . . the next three habits with the expression 'involve others in the problem and work out the solution together.'" This accurate but simple summary encompasses the many models, exercises, business cases, and examples (especially from his own family life) with which this dense but readable treasure is brimming.

Wayne W. Dyer, *The Power of Intention: Learning to Co-Create Your World Your Way* (Carlsbad, Calif.: Hay House, 2004)

Dr. Wayne Dyer, an internationally renowned author and speaker on self-development, follows up his bestselling *10 Secrets for Success and Inner Peace* with this examination of the nature of Intention. Dyer argues that Intention, a key aspect of self-coaching, is a force that is quite different from the dogged and sometimes painful determination that most of us would describe. Rather than being a product of our self-will, Dyer says, Intention is an inherent energy in the universe, present at our conception and available whenever we avoid the forces of ego and allow our connection with that energy to flourish. Dyer moves beyond theory to include practical steps for seeking the power of Intention and offers personal and professional examples of Intention at work in others' lives. Those who are seeking to incorporate a spiritual construct into their self-coaching work will be inspired and challenged. *Note:* This book has been showcased in a National Public Television special; look for DVDs and additional resources online at http://www.drwaynedyer.com.

Albert Ellis and Robert A. Harper, *A Guide to Rational Living* (New York: Institute for Rational Living, 1961)

Albert Ellis is hailed as one of the most influential psychologists of all time, and his book on rational living for the popular audience (originally published in 1961 and reissued in 1977) is a classic. Ellis is known as the founder of cognitive behavioral therapies (specifically, Rational Emotive Behavior Therapy, or REBT). His ideas are the basis for a huge proportion of clinical practice today.

Ellis has minimal interest in professionals' Freudian deconstruction of anguished childhoods. Without jargon, he encourages all who have the honesty needed for self-evaluation to engage in it. His radical view, evolved during the 1950s, is that human emotions "almost always include thoughts, attitudes, or beliefs, and can usually be distinctly changed by modifying our thinking." In short, we are agents in creating our own feelings—and in ridding ourselves of negative emotions.

Anyone who is undertaking a significant personal journey can expect to encounter land mines in the form of emotional barriers to change. A perusal of such chapters as "Reducing Your Dire Fears of Failure" and "How to Stop Blaming and Start Living" offer insightful, practical support for overcoming them.

Among Ellis's other numerous works are *Overcoming Destructive Beliefs, Feelings, and Behaviors* and *Dating, Mating, and Relating: How to Build a Healthy Relationship*.

Jared Fogle with Anthony Bruno, *Jared, the Subway Guy: Winning through Losing: 13 Lessons for Turning Your Life Around* (New York: St. Martin's Press, 2006)

This easy-reading reflection from the young man who lost 245 pounds on a self-designed regimen of low-fat sandwiches from the Subway chain is clearly labeled "Not a Diet Book!" and, indeed, it is not. Jared's hard-won perspective on overcoming negative behavior (eating, in his case) is a persuasive case study in the value of self-reliance and positive thinking. He offers practical advice on changing behavior for the long haul—including the importance of discarding the conventional wisdom in favor of forming a unique plan that works for you.

With no room for self-pity or lengthy psychoanalysis, Jared embodies the power of every individual's ability to access the change that he desires. However, in our experience, Jared's ability to reach his goal without any support is the exception rather than the rule. Although keeping his Intention secret until he had lost more than 100 pounds worked for Jared, it's a rare individual who can keep her goal in sight without the support of others.

John Gray, *How to Get What You Want and Want What You Have: A Practical and Spiritual Guide to Personal Success* (New York: HarperCollins, 1999)

According to his biography, John Gray is the "number one relationship author" in history. His bestselling *Men Are from Mars/ Women Are from Venus*, its sequels, and the associated seminars and products essentially redrew the feminist notion of minimizing the differences between men and women in order to gain equality. Instead, Gray's work on recognizing and embracing gender differences proved a door-opener for millions of couples.

In this later work, Gray addresses the limitations of achieving success in the internal or external arena only. He encourages us to recognize the interplay between achieving inner satisfaction while still experiencing our desire and passion for "more." Gray unapologetically entwines spiritual beliefs with sound psychological insights. Although he touts no specific theology, the practice of daily meditation is central to his thinking on achieving inner success: joy, peace, and happiness. Gray's view of "setting an intention" asks us to clearly state our personal objectives in order to free us up to receive what we desire. Also included is a detailed and practical discussion of removing our blocks to success by overcoming negative emotions—blame, anxiety, and 10 others—through well-described self-therapy techniques.

Phillip C. McGraw, *The Life Strategies Workbook: Exercises and Self-Tests to Help You Change Your Life* (New York: Hyperion, 2000)

If you're interested in looking more deeply into the unique psychological barriers that you face in achieving your goals, this workbook can give you the framework. It was written as a companion volume to the original *Life Strategies* by the psychologist known worldwide as "Dr. Phil." But the self-tests stand up on their own as a source of insight.

These inquiries cover nearly every aspect of life: health, work, family, and spiritual matters. McGraw's introductions to each section set the stage and suggest areas where you should be on the lookout. Here's a sampling of the exercises:

- The Rut Test, measuring the balance of action and inertia in your life (with a reminder that you "can't change what you don't acknowledge")
- The Perception Self-Test, identifying how your own filters affect your perception of a negative event
- What I Can Eliminate: 30 things (habits, relationships, assumptions, and so on) that you *don't* want in your life

Julie Morgenstern, *When Organizing Isn't Enough: SHED Your Stuff, Change Your Life* (New York: Fireside/Simon & Schuster, 2008)

Since her beginnings as a single mom and entrepreneur, Julie Morgenstern has climbed the ladder to become a guru-level consultant to individuals and corporations on organization and time management. Her books on these topics have hit the bestseller lists more than once. In this book, Morgenstern broadens her view of "clutter" to encompass not only physical possessions, but also schedules, obligations, and even behaviors that are holding us back. Or, as she writes, "By understanding and releasing your emotional attachments to tangible areas (like your space and schedule), SHED enables you to release intangible burdens including unhealthy beliefs, thoughts and behaviors." SHED is an acronym for the four-step plan that Morgenstern touts: Separate the treasures, Heave the trash, Embrace your identity, and Drive yourself forward.

While the author occasionally takes a bit too long to come to the point, the many case studies from her clients illustrate her points well. Little is lost by flipping to the topics that are most relevant to you; you can also explore her Web site, www.juliemorgenstern.com, to learn more about the SHED plan.

Eugene Pascal, *Jung to Live By: A Guide to the Practical Application of Jungian Principles for Everyday Life* (New York: Warner Books, 1992)

Any personal journey would probably be deepened by examining the principles of Carl Jung, the giant of twentieth-century psychological thought. In this book, Jungian analyst Eugene Pascal presents Jung's concepts to help nonprofessionals apply theory to real life.

From the author: "When our egos comprehend that the behaviors and attitudes of our psyches are just as real and as substantial as our physical bodies and that they constitute the personality that we are, we will come to understand why certain things always seem to happen to us. If we wish to change our destiny, we need to transform our character." The insight that you gain into your inner self and how it is expressed in your career choices, your relationships, and your preferences will help you clarify internal barriers and strengths that influence your success in attaining your objectives.

Steve Pavlina, *Personal Development for Smart People: The Conscious Pursuit of Personal Growth* (Carlsbad, Calif.: Hay House, 2008)

Steve Pavlina's wake-up call came early in life. At 18 years of age, he narrowly escaped imprisonment on felony charges, after he had developed a habit of stealing for the "rush" of the experience. Over the next few years, he took his life in hand, completing his education and launching a computer-game company, but the interest in personal development that drove him to turn his life around remained his passion. Over time, he has become the leading Internet blogger on personal development, attracting more than two million monthly readers.

This book, Pavlina's first, rejects the idea that self-improvement can be easily achieved through a single gimmick; instead, he outlines three core principles: truth, love, and power (and the adjunct principles derived from them: authority, oneness, and courage). Pavlina contends that embracing these principles through rigorous discipline defines the intelligent approach to personal growth. Pavlina includes advice for practical application of these principles to life's most challenging arenas: habits, career, money, health, relationships, and spirituality. Also see www.stevepavlina.com.

Eckhart Tolle, *The Power of Now: A Guide to Spiritual Enlightenment* (Vancouver, B.C., Canada: Namaste Publishing, 1997)

For the first year after its publication, the impact of Tolle's work on spiritual enlightenment grew from deliveries by hand to a few offbeat bookstores to a raging underground phenomenon, and then to receiving Oprah's praise, a place on the *New York Times* bestseller list (with sales in the millions of copies), and worldwide acceptance (translated into 33 languages).

Tolle's thoughts are presented in a conversational, question-and-answer format and are centered on "the transformation of consciousness," a transformation that is fundamental to attaining both personal happiness and the end of global conflict. As individuals, Tolle argues, we need to accept the power of Now, which he describes as "that intensely alive state that is free of time, free of problems, free of thinking, free of the burden of the personality." In this state, we can connect to "the eternal, ever-present One Life."

As a spiritual perspective on the barriers to happiness that our own egos create, *The Power of Now* has been transformative for a huge number of readers. Other Tolle works include *A New Earth* and *Stillness Speaks*.

www.selfimprovementbase.com

This Internet portal describes a wealth of resources available to people embarking on a self-help program, regardless of what area of their lives they are working on to improve. It includes books, articles, DVDs, audio programs, and Internet links.

GENERAL—ATTENTION DEFICIT DISORDER

Children and Adults with Attention Deficit/Hyperactivity Disorder (CHADD)

www.chadd.org

The CHADD organization is known to every professional who works with AD/HD children; it's the number one resource for parents, and also for adults who suspect that the cause of their own difficulties is more systemic than simple absentmindedness.

CHADD's programs are wide-ranging: a National Resource Center on AD/HD (www.help4adhd.org), an award-winning bimonthly magazine for members, and an online legislative action center for advocacy. Practical resources include a painstakingly researched yet easy to understand primer on the appropriate diagnosis and treatment of AD/HD. The Web site also helps association members and visitors identify resources in their area, including local CHADD affiliates. These groups offer support and ongoing education. When you've had your fill of the top-notch online material, look for a chapter in your area!

Edward M. Hallowell and John J. Ratey, *Driven to Distraction: Recognizing and Coping with Attention Deficit Disorder from Childhood through Adulthood* (New York: Simon & Schuster, 1994)

This work has been a national bestseller from its publication in 1994 until the present day. Drs. Hallowell and Ratey both admit to having ADD themselves. Hallowell proposed a collaboration to Ratey with the jest, "Do you think we can pay attention long enough to write a book?"

Far from giving a personal account, the authors draw instead on their vast clinical experience with children and adults: their struggles, their diagnoses, and the difference that appropriate treatment made in their lives. The result is an exceptionally practical and comprehensive book covering every aspect of living with ADD, from relationships with others, to self-organization, to moods and motivation.

It includes information on the various forms of ADD (both the well-known hyperactive type and other types characterized by inattention only). For those who are wondering if adult ADD may be causing their difficulties in following through on their intentions and goals, the sections that differentiate between ADD and other conditions (such as anxiety) are helpful, as are the explanations of ADD as a co-occurring characteristic (ADD and depression, ADD and creativity, and so on).

Kate Kelly and Peggy Ramundo, *You Mean I'm Not Lazy, Stupid or Crazy?! The Classic Self-Help Book for Adults with Attention Deficit Disorder* (New York: Scribner, 1993, 2006 update)

This reference book on attention deficit disorder (ADD) is written by two women who have ADD themselves. Their approach is open, warm, honest, and undeniably funny. Kelly and Ramundo easily empathize with the day-to-day struggles (and occasional triumphs) of men and women who may never have been diagnosed with ADD as children, but whose symptoms persist into adulthood.

The first chapters present accurate and comprehensive information on the diagnosis of ADD, its various forms, physiological causes, and the differences that a person with ADD manifests. Subsequent chapters look at the effect of ADD symptoms in life's various arenas: on the job, in the family, in friendships and intimate relationships, and in practical matters like preparing meals and organizing one's home. The final chapters talk about the potential benefits of both medication and meditation and about recognizing the warning signs of being overwhelmed.

Get ready to enjoy the authors' irreverent but helpful insights into "An ADD-Friendly Guide to Meditation," "Paper Pile Management," "Mealtime Mania," "Alternatives for Waking Up the Brain," and much more.

Nancy A. Ratey, *The Disorganized Mind: Coaching Your ADHD Brain to Take Control of Your Time, Tasks, and Talents* (New York: St. Martin's Press, 2008)

Adults with attention deficit/hyperactivity disorder (AD/HD) in any of its forms are likely to find self-coaching more challenging than others. Author and life coach Nancy Ratey knows all the pitfalls; she coped with her own undiagnosed AD/HD as a child through a structure imposed by her father but finally hit the wall in graduate school.

Ratey opens this book with an explanation of coaching and its particular value for people with AD/HD. She cites many client examples, acknowledging the special difficulties in maintaining an objective self-coaching awareness. Her systematic ANSWER model is applied to typical AD/HD symptoms: procrastination, impulsivity, time mismanagement, and the like. And she includes a brief section on the unique issues faced by those who live, love, and work with others who have AD/HD.

This is a simple, straightforward, but powerfully systematic approach to AD/HD coaching, with insights that can be useful to anyone working on similar challenges. It includes worksheets, a resource list, and excellent examples. Also see the Web site www.thedisorganizedmind.com, based on concepts from the book.

GENERAL—INTENTION

Daniel G. Amen, *Change Your Brain, Change Your Life: The Breakthrough Program for Conquering Anxiety, Depression, Obsessiveness, Anger, and Impulsiveness* (New York: Crown Publishing Group, 2010)

Psychiatrist Daniel Amen offers a fascinating look at the relationship between the physiological characteristics of the brain and the common psychological negatives that we encounter in ourselves and others: anxiety, depression, anger, and impulsiveness. Based on his work with brain-imaging techniques, Amen grew convinced that in many cases, the underlying cause was the physical structure or chemistry of the brain. The good news is that his continued research and clinical practice have also demonstrated that changes in those underlying causes are possible—and not always through surgery or medication. His approach to depression, for example, is centered on extinguishing ANTs (automatic negative thoughts).

Excellent examples and case histories are provided throughout, with insights into many negative behaviors (inattention, compulsive spending, panic attacks, and so on). Clear guidance is given concerning when and how to seek professional help. The personal, encouraging tone makes it clear that this professional's intent is to help every person maximize her brain function.

Also see Amen's follow-up volume, *Making a Good Brain Great*.

Joe Dispenza, *Evolve Your Brain: The Science of Changing Your Mind* [Dearfield, Fla.: Health Communications, Inc. (HCI), 2007]

This heady exploration of the brain is from Joe Dispenza, a biochemistry major and practicing chiropractor. His independent research into neurology and brain function was accelerated by a journey of personal healing that occurred when he suffered potentially paralyzing injuries, but nonetheless refused spinal surgery.

Dispenza's special interest is in understanding how the unhelpful chemical reactions in your brain, triggered by thoughts that keep you addicted to certain emotions, can be turned around. He succeeds in explaining the science of the brain in terms that are understandable for laypeople and draws some fascinating conclusions about our capacity for change.

Barbara Sher, *Wishcraft: How to Get What You Really Want*, 2nd ed. (New York: Viking Press, 1979; Ballantine Books, 2003)

Although this popular work long predates the current interest in life coaching, Sher was right on target, decades ahead of the pack. The two components of her thinking on achieving what you want in life are right in the title: to "Wish," or search for and identify what you really want to do, and "Craft," the skills that you'll need to accomplish your goal.

A series of exercises in the chapters on wishing are easily accomplished on your own; they help readers rediscover their own truest wishes and intentions. The next step in taking action on those intentions is brainstorming to overcome "I can't because . . ." barriers. And the additional skill of barn raising encourages you to get out your address book and throw a "resource party" to start gathering the information, contacts, and help that you'll need.

For more of Sher's practical insights on reinventing yourself, check out the bestselling *I Could Do Anything If I Only Knew What It Was* and *Refuse to Choose: A Revolutionary Program for Doing Everything That You Love*, published in 2006.

HEALTH

Michael F. Roizen and Mehmet C. Oz, *You, The Owner's Manual (Updated and Expanded Edition): An Insider's Guide to the Body That Will Make You Healthier and Younger* (Collins, 2005/HarperCollins, 2008)

This hefty tome kicks off with "The BQ Quiz: How Body Smart Are You?" That's an appropriate start for this book by two physicians that was based in part on a Discovery Channel series on health. Readers will painlessly gain detailed knowledge about their own body, with sections like "Your Pancreas: Sugar Smack" and "Leaky [coronary] Valves." Along the way, they'll find myths dispelled, factoids shared, and serious medical recommendations on the most important changes you can make to enjoy better and longer health. It's a thick but accessible book that deserves a spot on your coffee table for browsing, learning, and motivating.

RELATIONSHIPS

Mira Kirshenbaum, *Too Good to Leave, Too Bad to Stay: A Step-by-Step Guide to Help You Decide Whether to Stay In or Get Out of Your Relationship* (New York: Plume/Penguin, 1997)

This psychotherapist has captured guidelines, diagnostic questions, and supporting information and examples intended to help those who are seeking the right path forward in a frustrating relationship—in short, to stay or to go.

Straight talk, concise examples, and wisdom clearly born out of a commitment to the author's work with patients characterize this book. The journey you undertake in reading it is not an easy one, nor will it solve every relationship issue. But it will answer the question that Kirshenbaum frames here: are most people who respond to these same guidelines in a certain way happier if they leave their relationship? If you're wondering whether things are "too bad to stay," you can trust the answers you will find in this book.

WORK—CAREER CHANGE

Richard Bolles, *What Color Is Your Parachute?: A Practical Manual for Job-Hunters and Career-Changers* (Berkeley, Calif.: Ten Speed Press, annually since 1970)

With more than 10 million copies of this book on the street, and its legendary status as the gift of choice for the newly graduated or newly unemployed, this book needs little introduction.

The content here has been considerably expanded since the original editions of the early 1970s, which focused on assessing your own skills and mapping out what jobs were a good match. While that material is still included, Bolles has updated sections on interviews, résumés, salary negotiation, and starting your own business. The 2010 edition also highlights the current "hard times" and provides advice for the unemployed.

Checklists, diagrams, and many, many lists of references help you use this book as a self-coaching tool. And you'll understand how to access resources beyond this volume, including a 20-page listing of coaches across the United States.

Marty Nemko, *Cool Careers for Dummies,* 3rd ed. (Hoboken, N.J.: Wiley, 2007)

Still trying to figure out what you want to be? *Cool Careers for Dummies* includes quick introductions to "cool" careers, including many little-known ones.

Career expert Marty Nemko gives an overview of all the basics here as well: résumés, interviewing, career changing, and sections on the Top Ten Career Tips for Men, for Women, and "for Everyone." He presents alternative methods for finding jobs that require a college degree and those that do not. An interesting self-test, called "35 Most Revealing Questions about You," reframes the typical approach to matching your interests and aptitudes. Here, you'll be challenged to think about the types of people you like to be around, the things that make you angry (and whether you want to work on them in a career), and so on. The book is typical of those in the For Dummies series: approachable, humorous, and practical.

Cool Careers was the number-one-rated career guide in the Reader's Choice poll and reached number two on the *Wall Street Journal*'s National Business Bestseller list. Richard Bolles, author of *What Color Is Your Parachute?* writes this on the cover of the new edition: "Read this book. Use this book. You're in good hands. I guarantee you." *USA Today*'s review of the book called it "Full of smart advice."

Michael D. Watkins, *Your Next Move: The Leader's Guide to Navigating Major Career Transitions* (Boston: Harvard Business Press, 2009)

Michael Watkins is described as a "leadership transition guru." He also wrote the international bestseller *The First 90 Days*, which dealt with how managers and leaders can quickly get up to speed when they take on a new job or role.

In *Your Next Move*, Watkins homes in on eight specific kinds of career transition that you may face and how to ensure that change at work brings success. The scenarios described include promotion, joining a new company, leading former peers, and moving internationally, among others. For each scenario, he offers advice and tools for self-assessment and check-in. Count on this book to give you tips on reengineering your work relationships and tailoring your leadership style to meet the demands of transition challenges.

NETability, Inc.

http://www.job-hunt.org/

While it is overwhelming at first, this centralized Web resource for job searching is short on visual appeal but long on value, with thousands of links to trustworthy career advice, job opportunity sites, and useful tools. In fact, this site is an award winner, recognized by *U.S. News & World Report*, *Forbes*, and *PC Magazine* as a "top" or "best" Web site for job hunting and careers.

Take your time and browse deeply in the "Getting Started" section first; it offers excellent articles from career experts, links to additional targeted articles and guides, and a fine collection of "Online Job Hunting Basics." Two powerful facilities on the home page allow for a search of resources by state and an overall text search of articles on the site. Paid sponsors do have a column of advertisements, but they are well screened and useful. You can even follow Job-Hunt on Twitter.

There is something here for everyone, from baby boomers making close-to-retirement career changes to military veterans facing first-time entry into the job market. Whatever your situation, don't miss out on this alternative to combing through Monster.com listings.

WORK—NEW BUSINESS

Guy Kawasaki, *The Art of the Start: The Time-Tested, Battle-Hardened Guide for Anyone Starting Anything* (New York: Portfolio/Penguin, 2004)

Guy Kawasaki knows more than a little about start-ups. He's a bestselling author and sought-after speaker in the field. He now works as the managing director of Garage Technology Ventures (a venture capital group for high-tech entrepreneurs) and was the Apple Fellow charged with revitalizing the "Macintosh cult" in the mid-1990s.

His goal in this book is "to help you use your knowledge, love, and determination to create something great without getting bogged down in theory and unnecessary details." The start-up that you're embarking on may be a garage troupe of innovators, a division of a mega-firm launching a new product, or a not-for-profit organization; Kawasaki covers them all. In any case, he expects that you intend to change the world.

The Art of the Start covers all the basics: positioning, business planning, raising capital, branding, and, in a final chapter, "being a mensch." Yet the style is anything but business-school boring. In conversational, witty short takes, Kawasaki cuts to the heart of each start-up issue. His principles are complemented with charts of pithy examples, FAQs, and recommended reading. Make no mistake: you'll need more than one resource if you're in start-up mode, but this smart, concise work is a great place to begin.

Jan Norman, *What No One Ever Tells You about Starting Your Own Business: Real-Life Start-Up Advice from 101 Successful Entrepreneurs,* 2nd ed. (New York: Kaplan Publishing, 2004)

The premise of this book is a question that Jan Norman put to actual business owners: "If you could start all over again, what would you do differently to be more successful?" From the answers provided by men and women running companies, large and small, all over the United States, Norman has compiled (literally) 101 lessons for the prospective entrepreneur.

Most of these stories are only a page or two in length. Each one is focused on a particular event or situation that was unanticipated and that threatened the future of the business. Norman, a journalist who has covered small business for more than 20 years, organizes the stories into six logical sets of lessons: getting started, early decisions, funding, management, partners, and marketing.

This is a compact volume that's good for browsing; you'll be sure to discover at least one valuable lesson to benefit your own venture.

Useful Web Sites for Entrepreneurs, Spears School of Business, Entrepreneurship Program, Oklahoma State University

http://entrepreneurship.okstate.edu/nr/useful

Here's an interesting list of Web resources for entrepreneurs, assembled by members of the Entrepreneurship Program at the Spears School of Business. It includes links to a wide variety of government, academic, and private sites. Topics include venture capital, business plans, and marketing and e-commerce.

Harvard Business School sponsors a similar online resource at http://www.hbs.edu/entrepreneurship/resources.

Also see these commercially sponsored sites with excellent links:

- www.entrepreneur.com (*Entrepreneur* magazine)
- www.inc.com

INDEX

ABC model, 56
Ability, 24–26
Accurate data, 7–9, 114
Action stage, 13
Action steps:
ability, 38
briefing packet, 127–135
Circle of Support, 109–110
coachability, 36–41
discussion plan, 153
first step, 76
guide, 109
Intentions, 74–76
mapping your route, 181–183
permanency, 36–37
personal development plan, 182–183
planning, 181–183
readiness, 38–39
responding to feedback, 153
self-coachability, 39–41
setting objectives, 181–182
soliciting feedback, 127–135
stories, 75, 76
traveling companions, 109–110
Active listening, 141. *See also* Listening to the message
AD/HD, 237–240
ADD, 237–240
Addiction, 201
Additional resources for self-coachees, 219–247
addiction, generally, 219–220
alcohol addiction, 220–221
attention deficit disorder, 237–240
career change, 243–245
diet, 221–223
executive coaching, 226–227
gambling addiction, 223–224
general, 230–237
health, 242
Intention, 240–242
new business, 245–247
relationships, 242–243
self-coaching, 227–230
smoking, 224–226
spending, 224
Alcohol addiction, 220–221
Alcoholics Anonymous, 97–98, 220–221
ALS (Lou Gehrig's disease), 45–46, 71
Am I Hungry? What to Do When Diets Don't Work (May), 221
Amen, Daniel, 240, 241
American Lung Association, 224
Analyze feedback. *See* Responding to feedback
ANSWER model, 240
Ant and grasshopper story, Aesop's, 157
Aristotle, 46, 47
Art of the Start, The (Kawasaki), 245–246
Attending behavior, 141–143
Attention deficit disorder, 237–240

Barriers to success, 192–196
Basic principles, 5–7

Behavior, 21–23
Behavior-based feedback, 130–132
Berezinski, Tomasz, 106–107
Berry, Jo, 22
Body language, 142
Bolles, Richard, 243, 244
Briefing packet, 127–135
Browning, Robert, 160
Business coaching:
- barriers to success, 192–196
- denial, 139
- final reassessment, 209
- formal reassessment, 196–198
- gathering data, 114, 124
- go public, 34
- informal reassessment, 198–199
- mentor, 82–86
- PDP, 204
- presenting the Feedback Summary, 164
- questions not to ask, 119
- relapse, 201–202
- responding to feedback, 116
- soliciting feedback, 116, 117, 124
- stakeholders, 94–97, 204
- structured environment, 170–171
- time frame, 168–169

but, 71

Career change, 243–245
Carr, Allen, 224–225
Catastrophizing, 61, 67
Change Your Brain, Change Your Life (Amen), 240–241
Changing observable behavior, 209
Children and Adults with Attention Deficit/Hyperactivity Disorder (CHADD), 237–238
Churchill, Winston, 47
Circle of Support, 97–108
- action steps, 109–110
- biggest mistake, 108
- characteristics, 103
- extending the invitation, 101–102
- PDP, 204–205
- seven deadly sins, 107
- sources to consider, 105–106
- staying in touch, 200–201
- thank you, 211

Closing the loop, 150
Coach Anyone about Anything (Porche/Niederer), 229–230
Coach Yourself to Success (Miedaner), 228
Coachability, 17–41
- ability, 24–26
- action steps, 36–41
- behavior, 21–23
- permanency, 23–24
- readiness, 26–28
- willingness, 28–35

Coaching Quarterly Update, 198
Coaching the Mental Game (Dorfman), 227–228
Co-Active Coaching (Whitworth et al.), 227
Collaborative business partnerships, 113
Complexity, 160
Consciousness, 23, 48
Consequence-based suggestions, 134
Contemplation stage, 13, 27
Contingencies, 208
Continuous battle, 210–211
Cook, George, 108
Cool Careers for Dummies (Nemko), 243–244
Cooley, C. H., 81
Core limiting beliefs, 56
Counterfeit Intentions, 66–69
Creativity, 208
Cynic (inner voice), 72

Darwin, Charles, 201–202
Deadly inner voices, 72
Debtors Anonymous, 224
Decoding and feeding back feelings, 145–147
Denial, 139
Depersonalization, 26, 31, 164
Developing your plan. *See* Mapping your route
DiClemente, Carlo, 13, 26–27
Diet, 221–223

Discussion Plan, 150–153
Disorganized Mind: Coaching Your ADHD Brain to Take Control of Your Time, Tasks, and Talents, The (Ratey), 239–240
Dispenza, Joe, 241
Divine Comedy (Dante), 80
"Dr. Phil," 234
Driven to Distraction: Recognizing and Coping with Attention Deficit Disorder from Childhood through Adulthood (Hallowell/Ratey), 238–239
Drop your defenses, 31
Dyer, Wayne, 48, 51, 70, 232

Easy Way to Stop Smoking, The (Car), 224–225
Eat This, Not That 2010! The No-Diet Weight Loss Solution (Zinczenko/Goulding), 223
Eat What You Love, Love What You Eat (May), 221
Ego ideal, 140
Ellis, Albert, 7, 25, 33, 55, 56, 232
Emerson, Ralph Waldo, 207
Entrepreneurship Program (Spears School of Business), 247
Erhard, Werner, 51, 68, 231
erhard seminars training (est), 213–214, 230–231
est (erhard seminars training): 60 Hours That Transform Your Life (Bry), 230–231
Evolve Your Brain: The Science of Changing Your Mind (Dispenza), 241
Executive coaching. *See* Business coaching
Exercises. *See* Action steps
Expect the unexpected, 206
Explicit environment, 59

Failure, 207
Fatalist (inner voice), 72
Feedback:
  defined, 115
  gift, as, 31
  reassessment, 203
  responding to. *See* Responding to feedback
  sample, 148
  soliciting. *See* What's the message
  types, 131–132
Feedback Questionnaire, 118, 127
Feedback Summary, 113–114
Feeding back emotions, 146
Filters, 145
First 90 Days, The (Watkins), 244
Follow-up interview, 147
Ford, Henry, 207
Formal assessment, 196–198
Franklin, Benjamin, 208
Freudians, 24

Gambling addiction, 223–224
Gestures, 142
Getting and staying there, 187–211
  arrival, 208–210
  capture the changes, 204–205
  continuous battle, 210–211
  feedback, 203
  need to reassess, 190–196
  reassessment, 196–201
  relapse, 201–203
  rethinking your Intention, 205–206
  rules of the road, 206–208
  thank you, 211
Getting Things Done (Allen), 230
Go public, 34
Going-in stories, 55–59
Golden Rule, 130
Goldsmith, Marshall, 226
Gray, John, 234
Greene, Bob, 3, 104
GTD phenomenon, 230
Guide, 9–11, 86–94
  action steps, 109
  author's example, 88–89
  biggest mistake, 108
  biweekly reassessment, 200
  caveats, 90–91
  characteristics, 86–88, 91
  example (Tom), 89–90

Guide *(Continued)*
planning meeting, 164, 178–180
roles/responsibilities, 87
shadow coach, as, 149, 164
sources to consider, 91–92
thank you, 211
tips/hints, 92–93
what to do, 93
who it shouldn't be, 89
Guide to Rational Living, A (Ellis), 232–233
Guiding principles, 5–7

Health, 242
Heart attack victims, 201
Herman Goelitz Candy Company, 79
Hillary, Edmund, 80
Hitler, Adolf, 47
Hold fast, 207
Hopkins, Anthony, 225
Hot spots, 20
How to Get What You Want and Want What You Have (Gray), 233–234

I Could Do Anything If I Only Knew What It Was (Sher), 242
Implementing the plan. *See* Getting there
Implicit environment, 58
Indiana Jones and the Last Crusade, 19
Influencing others, 168
Informal assessment, 198–199
Inner critic, 25
Inner critic (inner voice), 72
Inner voice, 70–72
Intention. *See* Setting your Intention
Intention-busting stories, 64
Intention-focused, 160
Intention-setting process, 50
International Coach Federation (ICF), 226
Interview:
follow-up, 147
listening to, 149
personal, 124–125, 147
Irrational beliefs, 33, 56

James, William, 203
Jared, "the Subway Guy," 10
Jared, the Subway Guy (Fogle/Bruno), 233
Jelly Belly Candy Company, 79
Joyner-Kersee, Jackie, 53
Jump into action, 65–66, 76

Kafka, Franz, 160
Khayyam, Omar, 62
King, Gayle, 104
KISS mode, 160

Law of compensation, 208
Leadership, 113
Leadership presence, 168
Leading questions, 119
Leap of faith, 19
Lennon, John, 206
Leonard, Thomas J., 228
Lewis and Clark (explorers), 80
Life Strategies Workbook, The (McGraw), 234–235
Listening to the message, 141–147
attending behavior, 141–143
decoding and feeding back feelings, 145–147
paraphrasing, 144
passive listening, 143
say more responses, 144
Lodwick, Todd, 206
Looking-glass self, 81
Lou Gehrig's disease (ALS), 45–46, 71

MacLeish, Archibald, 71
Maintenance stage, 14
Making It All Work: Winning at the Game of Work and the Business of Life (Allen), 230
Mapping your route, 155–185
action steps, 181–183
Aesop's ant and grasshopper story, 157

communicating your progress, 173, 178, 183
example (Steve), 168–170
PDP. *See* Personal development plan (PDP)
planning meeting, 163–164, 178–180
planning pillars, 160–162
rationalizations for failure, 158–159
setting objectives, 165–167, 181–182
watch-outs, 170–172
www.coachyourselftowin.com, 163
May, Michelle, 221
McClure, Jennifer B., 4
Memorandum, 128–129
Mentor, 82–86. *See also* Guide
characteristics, 82–83
examples, 84–85
shadow coach, as, 84
who it usually is, 83
Miller, Patricia, 108
Mirroring, 144
Mojo: How to Get It, How to Keep It, and How to Get It Back If You Lose It (Goldsmith), 226
Monitoring your progress. *See* Getting and staying there
Montaigne, Michel de, 81
Morgenstern, Julie, 235
Murphy's Law, 161, 191

National Clearinghouse for Alcohol and Drug Information, 219
National Council on Problem Gambling, 223–224
National Eating Disorders Association, 222
Negative feedback, 131
Negative feedforward, 132
Negative inner voice, 70, 72
NETability, Inc., 245
New business, 245–247
"New You" stories, 63–64, 76
Nidetch, Jean, 4
Night watchman (inner voice), 72
Nonverbal behavior, 142

Observed behavior, 130–131, 132
Odyssey (Homer), 82, 189
Orr, Bobby, 52
Outer voice, 70
Overgeneralization, 60
Oz, Mehmet, 104

Parachute, 208
Paraphrasing, 144
Pascal, Blaise, 49
Passion, 49
Passive listening, 143
Pavlina, Steve, 236
PDP. *See* Personal Development Plan (PDP)
Permanency, 23–24
Personal Development for Smart People (Pavlina), 236
Personal Development Plan (PDP):
action step, 182–183
example (Keely J.), 172–173, 174–177
making changes to, 204
overview, 149
template, 184–185
Personal interview, 124–125, 147
Peter Principle, 192
Planning. *See* Mapping your route
Planning meeting, 163–164, 178–180
Planning pillars, 160–162
Pollyanna (inner voice), 72
Portable Coach: 28 Surefire Strategies for Business and Personal Success, The (Leonard), 228
Positive feedback, 132
Positive feedforward, 132
Post-interview conduct, 147
Power of Intention: Learning to Co-Create Your World Your Way, The (Dyer), 48, 232
Power of Now, The (Tolle), 237
Power of Self-Coaching, The (Luciani), 229
Precontemplation stage, 13
Preparation stage, 13
Prochaska, James O., 13, 26–27
Procrastinator (inner voice), 72

Racketeer (inner voice), 72
Rational emotive behavior therapy (REBT), 25, 33–34
Rationalizer (inner voice), 72
Readiness, 26–28
Ready for Anything: 52 Productivity Principles for Work and Life (Allen), 230
Reagan, Ronald, 79
Realism, 134–135, 160
Reassessment, 196–201
REBT, 25, 33–34
Recidivism, 201
Reframe your stories, 32–33
Refuse to Choose (Sher), 242
Reik, Theodor, 140
Relapse, 201–203
Relationships, 242–243
Resilience, 162
Responding to feedback, 137–153
  action step, 153
  analyzing the data, 147–149
  business coaching, 116
  closing the loop, 150
  constructing the plan, 149
  discussion plan, 150–153
  listening, 141–147. *See also* Listening to the message
  post-interview conduct, 147
Responsible victim, 30
Rethinking your Intention, 205–206
Routine, 207
Rowland, Herm, 79
Rules of the road, 206–208

Say more responses, 144
SBA, 80
SCORE (Service Corps of Retired Executives), 80
Searching for Safety (Wildavsky), 162
Self-coaching:
  action steps. *See* Action steps
  coachability. *See* Coachability
  implementing the plan. *See* Getting and staying there
  Intention. *See* Setting your Intention
  planning. *See* Mapping your route
  preconditions, 7–15
  responding to feedback. *See* Responding to feedback
  roles/responsibilities, 87
  soliciting feedback. *See* What's the message
  steps in process, 15–16
  taking the first step, 65–66, 76
  travel companions. *See* Travel companions
Self Coaching (Luciani), 229
selfimprovementbase.com, 92, 237
Self-reflection, 20, 29
Service Corps of Retired Executives (SCORE), 80
Setting objectives, 165–167, 181–182
Setting your Intention, 43–76
  action steps, 74–76
  consciousness, 48
  counterfeit Intentions, 66–69
  declare your Intention again, 66
  famous mottos, 47
  Intention, defined, 46–47
  jump into action, 65–66
  keeping your Intention strong, 69–73
  passion, 49
  rethinking your Intention, 205–206
  Step 1 (write down your Intention), 50
  Step 2 (declare Intention to others), 50–52
  Step 3 (begin living in your Intention), 52–55
  Step 4 (uncover your stories), 55–60
  Step 5 (reevaluate your stories), 60–61
  Step 6 (payoffs/costs), 61–63
  Step 7 (create new stories), 63–64
7 Habits of Highly Effective People, The (Covey), 231
Seven Steps to breakthrough performance, 15–16, 211
Shadow coach, 84, 149, 164

SHED, 235
Sher, Barbara, 241, 242
Silence, 143
Simmons, Richard, 4
Simplicity, 20
Sisyphus, 23
Small Business Administration (SBA), 80
"Small Wins" (Weick), 162
SMART objectives, 165–167, 181–182
smokefree.gov, 225–226
Smoking, 27, 224–226
SOLER model of attending behavior, 142, 143
Soliciting feedback. *See* What's the message
Spending (addiction), 224
Stages of behavior change, 13–14
Stakeholders, 94–97, 204. *See also* Circle of Support
Starting up, 65–66, 76
Stories:
- action steps, 75, 76, 181
- going-in, 55–59
- Intention-busting, 64
- New You, 63–64, 76
- payoffs/costs, 61–62, 76
- planning, and, 158, 159, 181
- reassessment, and, 194–195
- reevaluation, 60–61
- reframing, 32–33
- uncovering, 55–60

Stress, 194
Substance Abuse and Mental Health Services Administration, 219
Suggest, don't direct, 134
Sustained behavioral change, 23

Taking the first step, 65–66, 76
Thank you, 211
Theme, 148
360-degree feedback, 125
Three-part model, 131
Time lines, 161
Tolle, Eckhart, 20
Too Good to Leave, Too Bad to Stay (Kirshenbaum), 242–243
"Track changes" feature, 204
Track your success and recalibrate. *See* Getting and staying there
Transtheoretical model of change, 13–14
Traveling companions, 77–110
- action steps, 109–110
- Circle of Support. *See* Circle of Support
- famous examples, 80
- guide. *See* Guide
- mentor, 82–86
- stakeholders, 94–97
- why important, 81

Triathlon, 99–100, 200
Twelve-step "anonymous" programs, 220
28 Laws of Attraction: Stop Chasing Success and Let It Chase You, The (Leonard), 228

Uncertainty, 19

Vera Bradley Designs, 108
Victim, 30
Vocabulary of uncertainty, 70–71

Watch-outs, 170–172
Web sites. *See* Additional resources for self-coachees
Weick, Karl, 162
Weight Watchers, 97–98
Weight Watchers International, 222–223
Weight Watchers Mobile, 222–223
Weight Watchers Online, 222
What Color Is Your Parachute? (Bolles), 243
What Got You Here Won't Get You There (Goldsmith), 226
What-ifs, 160–161
What No One Ever Tells You about Starting Your Own Business (Norman), 246

What's the message, 111–135
  action steps, 127–135
  briefing packet, 127–135
  business coaching, 116
  collecting the data, 124–126
  feedback, defined, 115
  framing the questions, 117–124
  generic questions, 119–120
  guidelines for delivering feedback, 129–135
  leading questions, 119
  memorandum, 128–129
  questionnaire, 118, 127
  sample Feedback Questionnaire, 118
  sample Feedback Summary, 113–114
  sample questions, 120–124
  soliciting feedback, 115–116
When Organizing Isn't Enough: SHED Your Stuff, Change Your Life (Morgenstern), 235–236
Wildavsky, Aaron, 162
Williamson, Marianne, 104
Willingness, 12–14, 28–35
Winfrey, Oprah, 3, 68, 104
Wions, Joe, 45–46, 71, 72
Wishcraft: How to Get What You Really Want (Sher), 241–242
Writing down your plan, 162
www.selfimprovementbase.com, 92, 237

You Mean I'm Not Lazy, Stupid or Crazy?! The Classic Self-Help Book for Adults with Attention Deficit Disorder (Kelly/Ramundo), 239
Your Next Move: The Leader's Guide to Navigating Major Career Transitions (Watkins), 244
You, The Owner's Manual (Roizen/Oz), 242

ABOUT THE AUTHOR

Howard M. Guttman is principal of Guttman Development Strategies, Inc. (GDS), a Mount Arlington, New Jersey-based management consulting firm founded in 1989 and specializing in executive coaching; building horizontal, high-performance teams; strategic and organizational alignment; and management development training (www.guttmandev.com). GDS has been ranked as a top leadership development consulting firm by *Leadership Excellence* magazine, which also named Mr. Guttman to its list of "Excellence 100 Top Thought Leaders."

Among GDS's U.S. and international corporate clients are Bloomberg LP; Colgate-Palmolive; John Hancock; Johnson & Johnson; L'Oréal USA; Mars, Inc.; Novartis; Pfizer; and Walmart.

Mr. Guttman is the author of *Great Business Teams: Cracking the Code for Standout Performance* (John Wiley; www.greatbusinessteams.com), named one of the Top Business Books of 2008 by Soundview Executive Book Summaries. He is also the author of *When Goliaths Clash: Managing Executive Conflict to Build a More Dynamic Organization*. His third book, *Coach Yourself to Win: Seven Steps to Breakthrough Performance on the Job and in Your Life*, is based on the proven process that he and his consultants have used to coach thousands of executives in major organizations around the world to higher levels of performance.

Mr. Guttman is quoted frequently in the business press and in broad-interest magazines and newspapers such as *TIME* magazine, *The Washington Post*, *U.S. News and World Report*, *U.S.A. Today* magazine, and *Investors Business Daily*. He is also a frequent contributor to professional journals such as *Harvard Management Update, Human Resource Executive, Chief Executive,* and *Leader to Leader.*

Mr. Guttman is a sought-after speaker who addresses corporate and academic audiences on such topics as "Executive Coaching: Lessons from the Firing Line," "Great Business Teams: What Does It Take?", "Conflict Management as a Core Leadership Competency," "Putting Performance into High-Performance Teams," and "Alignment: Creating High-Performance Teams from the Top Down."